Anonymous

Incidents on Land and Water

Four Years on the Pacific Coast

Anonymous

Incidents on Land and Water
Four Years on the Pacific Coast

ISBN/EAN: 9783744649438

Printed in Europe, USA, Canada, Australia, Japan

Cover: Foto ©Andreas Hilbeck / pixelio.de

More available books at **www.hansebooks.com**

INCIDENTS ON LAND AND WATER,

Four Years on the Pacific Coast.

BEING A NARRATIVE OF THE

BURNING OF THE SHIPS NONANTUM, HUMAYOON AND FANCHON, TOGETHER WITH MANY STARTLING AND INTERESTING ADVENTURES ON SEA AND LAND.

BY

MRS. D. B. BATES.

EIGHTH EDITION.

BOSTON.
PUBLISHED FOR THE AUTHOR.
1860.

Entered, according to Act of Congress, in the year 1857, by
MRS. D. B. BATES,
in the Clerk's Office of the District Court of the District of Massachusetts

INTRODUCTION.

Kind Reader! This simple unembellished history of portions of my life's experience requires no preface. Its deficiencies, I trust, will save it from unjust criticisms; if justly deserved, may they be in all lenity bestowed, modified by sympathy, and kindness for the humble historian.

CONTENTS.

CHAPTER I.
My Childhood's Home, ... 11

CHAPTER II.
The Departure, ... 12

CHAPTER III.
Fire on board Ship Nonantum at Sea, ... 17

CHAPTER IV.
The Falkland Islands, ... 23

CHAPTER V.
A South Sea Rookery, ... 39

CHAPTER VI.
Departure from the Falklands, and second fire off Cape Horn, . 45

CHAPTER VII.
Third fire at sea. Burning of the Ship Fanchon on the Coast of Peru, ... 57

CHAPTER VIII.

The Desolate Beach, ... 68

CHAPTER IX.

Arrival and Residence at Payta, ... 73

CHAPTER X.

Arrival at Panama and visit Taboga, ... 82

CHAPTER XI.

Arrival at San Francisco. Extensive Conflagration. Its Consequences, etc., etc., ... 96

CHAPTER XII.

Leave San Francisco for Marysville, ... 111

CHAPTER XIII.

Situation and Climate of Marysville. Peep at the Country, Inhabitants, etc. 125

CHAPTER XIV.

Hotel Keeping and Life in a Canvas Shanty, . . . 137

CHAPTER XV.

Description of an Indian Rancheria and its Occupants, . . 149

CHAPTER XVI.

A Conflagration. Hotel Keeping resumed. Marysville Inundated, ... 156

CONTENTS.

CHAPTER XVII.

A Journey up the Sacramento Valley. Descriptions of things seen and heard, ... 163

CHAPTER XVIII.

Trip to French Corral. Mountain Scenery. Mountain Ball, etc. 169

CHAPTER XIX.

Journey to Park's Bar. Experience in Mining. Fatal results of Gambling, ... 192

CHAPTER XX.

Visit to Gen. Sutter's residence. Description of the grounds. The Pleasant Surprise, or the Musical Miner. Good Fortune of a Lady in California. Emigrant Wagons. Belles of the Plain. Interesting and Ludicrous Incident. The English Gold Diggers. Loss of Life, ... 205

CHAPTER XXI.

The Orphan Child. Delights of Stage-Coaching in California. The Hen that laid the Golden Eggs, ... 222

CHAPTER XXII.

Execution of a man in Marysville. The petty theft the results of bad Influence. Accident at the Mines. "Obstinate as a Mule." Mysterious Disappearance of Dunbar. Cold Blooded Murder. Disinterested Benevolence, ... 232

CHAPTER XXIII.

Hardships of the Mountain Settlers during the winter of 1852. A Brother's Experience, ... 254

CHAPTER XXIV.

Peculiarities of John Chinaman. Conflagration in Marysville, . 263

CHAPTER XXV.

Farewell to Marysville. Departure. Arrival at San Francisco. Leave San Francisco for Home, ... 271

CHAPTER XXVI.

Incidents of the passage. Burial at Sea, ... 275

CHAPTER XXVII.

Arrival at Panama. Description of Hotels. Walks about the city. The Battlement, ... 283

CHAPTER XXVIII.

Crossing the Isthmus. Grave by the road-side. The beautiful Valley of Obispo. Take the cars for Aspinwall, . . . 291

CHAPTER XXIX.

Embark for Home, on board the North Star. A distressed family, 307

CHAPTER XXX.

Arrival at New York, ... 314

CHAPTER XXXI.

Incidents illustrative of Morals in California, ... 315

CHAPTER XXXII.

Conclusion, ... 334

INCIDENTS ON LAND AND WATER.

CHAPTER I.

In the town of Kingston, in the State of Massachusetts, not many miles distant from that ancient and time-honored bay whose waters years ago kissed the prow of the "May Flower" as she approached a sterile and inhospitable shore, is situated the home of my childhood.

The dear old homestead, the scene of so many fond recollections, had descended from father to son for generations. The storms of many winters had beaten upon its roof; time had left its impress without, in the shape of moss-covered shingles; but within, all was youthful joy and gladness. Not a link in that family circle had been severed. In love and affection were we nurtured.

Although years have intervened since those sunny days of childhood, how often, while sojourning in distant lands, would memory recall with undimmed freshness the gladsome spring-time of youth. Happy days! too speedily do they fly, leaving, often, nought but the recollection of them to cheer us in our toilsome march. Early in life, I was united to one whose home was on the deep. Then came the sad partings from loved friends, to follow for many consecutive years the fortunes of my husband by sea and land. There were sad departures and joyful returns.

CHAPTER II.

On the 27th of July, 1850, I sailed from Baltimore in the ship *Nonantum*, of Boston, (Bates, master,) bound to San Francisco. In the ship's hold was stowed one thousand and fifty tons of coal; the between-decks were filled with provisions for the steamers plying between Panama and the El Dorado of the West. The coal with which we were laden was taken from the Cumberland mines, brought directly to Baltimore in open iron cars, subject to frequent showers of rain on the way, and deposited in that condition in the ship.

With bright hopes and glowing anticipations we left our native land. Well was it that no prophetic visions presaged the future that awaited us. We were wholly unconscious at the time of the remarks uttered by the spectators assembled upon the wharf, to the effect that coal was a dangerous cargo to take upon so long a voyage.

By the lessons taught by the bitter experiences of that memorable year, many shipmasters have duly profited. Now, they stow their coal in casks, or in small quantities, have it dry when placed on board, and give it sufficient ventilation.

The ship's crew consisted of the usual complement of sailors, first and second officers, carpenter, cook, and steward; also two boys, who particularly attracted my attention. They were pleasant little fellows, who, being possessed of a mania for the sea, had left their homes to seek their fortunes upon the treacherous deep. Many times during the voyage had they occasion to bless the captain's wife for a bite of something good from the cabin table, slyly given to them, and in secret eaten.

This was not my first voyage. To me the cabin of a wave-tossed vessel, and a trip across the deep green ocean, was never monotonous or disagreeable, never being afflicted with that unpleasant nausea termed "sea-sickness," so much to be dreaded, judging from the appearance and descriptions received. The separation from earth's homes and loved hearts are all calculated to elevate the mind, and centre the soul's best affections upon pure and holy objects. How often, hour after hour, have I sat gazing upon the boundless expanse of water, contrasting in my mind the utter insignificance of human power and skill, compared with the majesty of the Almighty Maker of the ocean and the land.

Moonlight nights at sea are my especial delight. How I love to gaze upon the illimitable deep, and watch each ripple gleaming and sparkling in the broad and trackless pathway like myriads of diamonds beneath the effulgent beams of the glorious orb of night! Almost imperceptibly, a holy calm pervades my being, and absorbs all other faculties. With what reluctant feelings, on such evenings as these, would I resign my seat upon deck, even after the night was far spent.

Before leaving Baltimore, my husband had purchased a beautiful Newfoundland dog, of the largest species; to which, on account of the remarkable sagacity he displayed, I became very much attached. In my daily promenade upon deck, he was ever by my side. Whenever a sail was discovered in the distance, he would place his huge fore-paws on the ship's rail, and send his loud, hoarse bark reverberating far over the swelling wave.

Then I had two goats on board to furnish milk, not being sailor enough to drink the strong coffee made on ship-board. They were very playful, and once a day were allowed the liberty of the deck, which they readily improved by racing and frolicking about, in which they were joined by Dash.

In pleasant weather, when off the coast of Brazil, I have sat for hours on the ship's rail fishing for albatross, one of the largest and most formidable of the South Sea birds, as they majestically sailed along in the wake of the ship, watching the bait (a piece of pork fastened to the hook, and a small bit of board attached to the line to float it,) so temptingly displayed. After swallowing it, and finding themselves captured, there was no struggling to free themselves, but, as you hauled in the line, they would sail gracefully along in all their native beauty and dignity. The assistance of the two boys was required in bringing them to the deck, where, after freeing them from the hook, (which, the boys always assured me, did not hurt them in the least,) they would survey the scene around them with a sort of contemptuous glance, as though they disdained their captors and the deception used to allure them from their native element. The goats, when freed from their inclosures, would advance towards them, rear themselves on their hind-legs, and shake their heads in defiance of the monster bird; while it, in turn, would snap its tremendous bill with such force, you could hear it ring from one part of the ship to the other; but they would never encounter one another except by threatening gestures. When we became satisfied with admiring our prisoner, two sailors would each grasp a wing, raise him to the side of the ship, give him a toss, and away he would soar; then light gracefully upon the water at a little distance, and view what I suppose he thought to be a huge monster which had held him in his grasp.

Another amusement was taking a dish of crumbs, and, by throwing over a handful, call a flock of cape-pigeons to the ship's side. Each one eager to secure his share, they would dive far down into the clear water to get those that were sinking. Sometimes, to deceive them, I would throw over a bone that would sink rapidly. Down they would all go after it out of sight; then appear again, chattering, —scolding, I called the incessant noise they kept up. This bird resembles our tame pigeon, with the exception of being a little larger.

Flocks of "Mother Carey's chickens" were occasionally following in our wake. Those tiny little things, ever on the wing, often excited my sympathy. About this time, the faithful dog I had learned to love so well sickened, and daily grew worse. Every remedy we could devise was called into requisition, but availed nought. One night, after I had retired, he dragged himself to my berth, placed his nose close to my face, and whined and moaned piteously. I afterwards thought it prophetic of evil in the future. Upon making my appearance upon deck the next morning, there lay the noble animal dead. Poor old Dash! the remembrance of thee and thy many virtues will live long on memory's leaf.

CHAPTER III.

Days and weeks passed on, until we were in the latitude of the Rio de la Plata. So mild and pleasant had been the weather, that I was half inclined to believe this voyage indeed was to be an exception to all previous ones; although often, when expressing myself delighted with the continuance of such lovely weather, the exuberance of my feelings would be somewhat checked by repeated assurances from my husband that I should see it "rough enough" off Cape Horn to compensate for all previous calms.

Suddenly the aspect of affairs changed, and we encountered a terrific storm, the bare recollection of which almost makes me shudder. The ship's cabin was a house upon deck; and, as the storm increased in violence, the angry waves dashing higher and higher as each successive blast lashed the mighty deep, fears were entertained that the house would be forcibly detached from the deck. Heavy shutters were fastened against the windows as a protection to the glass against the storm, thereby rendering the cabin dark as night. A lantern was kept burning through the day, as well as by night. Owing to the violent motion of the ship, I was compelled, for the most part of the time, to keep my berth, to prevent being dashed against the cabin walls. I very reluctantly consented to confine myself to my state-room, but not, however, until I had received some severe bumps. So violent and sudden were those jerks, that, unless one was very much guarded, they would be thrown very unceremoniously from their seat.

Oh, it was terrible to lie so many hours listening to the roaring of the storm without! I wished very much to get a glimpse of the ocean when lashed into such fury, but there was no aperture whereby I could gratify my curiosity. I had only to pray, and listen alone. My husband was constantly on deck, taking neither refreshment nor sleep. I wondered not at his anxiety, although I knew not then the imminent danger impending from fire as well as water; for, the second morning after the commencement of the storm, smoke had been discovered between decks. The alarming truth instantly flashed upon our minds. The gas that originated from the coal had generated fire. Orders were immediately given to get up provisions and water sufficient to last until we could be released from our awful situation. While thus engaged, several of the men were rendered senseless from the effects of the gas. They next proceeded to close the hatches, and caulked every seam tightly, in the hope of arresting the progress of the fire it was impossible to extinguish.

Captain B—— shaped his course for the nearest

land — the Falkland Islands, which were eight hundred miles distant. During this time, the severity of the gale was such, it compelled me to remain in the cabin; and for three days I remained in ignorance of our perilous situation. During this interval, the air in the cabin was ever impregnated with a strong odor of tar. This was accounted for to me in this light, — the cook was boiling tar, as they were obliged to make use of a great deal at such times. That, of course, looked very reasonable, and served the purpose of concealment from me of the fire. It is true the countenances of my husband and officers bore unmistakable traces of anxiety; but this I readily attributed to the violence of the gale, which threatened every moment to engulf us.

I also noticed the steward caulking some of the seams in the pantry. Upon inquiry, he gave me to understand it was necessary to use this precaution, to prevent any liquids he should chance to spill from running down on the cargo, — a foolish excuse, to be sure; but, however, it proved effective. But, when the gas and smoke escaped through seams which were apparently water-tight, and made its appearance in the cabin, concealment was no longer possible.

Upon learning the sad truth, for a time all fortitude and self-control forsook me. I thought of my dear old home far away, in its quiet seclusion; of the loved ones wont to assemble there to talk and pray for the safety of the absent one. I felt I should never more behold them, and that they would ever remain in ignorance of our fate. After the first moments of despair, Hope again asserted her empire. Repinings, I reasoned, were useless. The Almighty hand which formed the channels of the deep had power, I knew, to preserve us, and guide us, amidst storm and darkness, to our homes and havens of rest. The greatest consternation prevailed among the crew. At times the gale would abate, only to be renewed with increased violence. We were soon obliged to vacate the cabin, which was filled to suffocation with gas; and, for five consecutive days and nights, I remained in a chair which was lashed to the deck. It was quite cold, and often I was drenched with the water and spray that would dash at short intervals across the deck. Never can I forget those dreary days of suffering that I sat gazing from the narrow deck upon the boundless expanse of tossing, foam-crested billows. As far as eye could reach, no friendly sail appeared to which we could look for safety; nothing was seen but the sweeping surge, as it came roaring and dashing on, threatening to overwhelm us. In such an hour man learns of God, and witnesses proof of his grandeur and power in every dashing wave; he sees nature in one of its grandest aspects.

If possible, the nights exceeded in anxiety the days; impenetrable darkness surrounded us, relieved only by sheets of white foam dashing over the bows, as the doomed ship madly plunged into the angry waters. When one sea more powerful than another would strike her, causing her to tremble in every timber, I would grasp my chair, shut my eyes, and think we were fast being engulfed in the sea. Oh, those nights of agony! Never, through all the vicissitudes of after life, will one thought, one feeling, then endured, fade from the volume of memory.

Each day the ship was getting hotter; gas and smoke were escaping at every seam. We constantly feared an explosion, as the natural consequence of so much confined gas. What a solace to me, in those days of trial, was the trust, the implicit confidence, I felt in that mighty Guardian Power that is ever around and about us, and in whose protection we are forever safe!

On the twelfth day after fire was first discovered, we made the Falkland Islands. As we approached the Volunteer Rocks, which make off two miles from land, gloomy and forbidding as were their appearance, I hailed them as harbingers of safety. Truly it must have been the sunshine, the grateful happiness of the heart, which clothed those barren rocks with imaginary beauty — I had almost said reverence.

CHAPTER IV.

THE entrance to the outer bay is called Port William. About twenty miles up this bay, an English colony is established. The entrance to Port William is designated by a tall flag-staff. At the time of our arrival, it was blowing a close-reefed-topsail breeze, directly down the bay; and, as night was approaching, the captain deemed it advisable to select the most sheltered situation at hand, and anchor until morning.

Formerly, this colony was located up Berkley's Sound, and called Port Louis. It has since been removed to its present site, and styled Port Stanley. The Falkland Islands are situated in the South Atlantic Ocean, where the mariner guides his course at night by the sacred constellation of the Southern Cross, and between the parallels of 51 deg. and 53 deg. south, and extending from 57 deg. to nearly 62 deg. west. The only two of considerable size are the East and West Falkland. These are separated by a channel. Around these islands are numerous rocks, whose distance from the shores, where tides run strongly, and winds are violent as well as sudden, renders it rather difficult to navigate. In approaching land, and particularly when entering a harbor, a good look-out should be kept for fixed kelp, which grows upon every rock covered by the sea, and not far below the surface. Lying upon the water, the leaves and stalk serve as well as a buoy to warn of hidden danger. A region more exposed to storms, both in summer and winter, it would be difficult to mention. High winds are prevalent, and very violent at times. During the summer, a calm day is an extraordinary event. Generally speaking, the nights are less windy than the days. Altogether, the appearance of these lonely isles of the South are dismal and uninviting in the extreme. Moorland and black bog extend in nearly every direction; although there are valleys affording coarse, excellent grass, upon which thousands of wild cattle subsist. Some tracts of land, I was informed, at the southern part of the island, were low, level, and abundantly productive of excellent herbage. Many years since, the French and Spanish left, at different times, cattle and horses upon the isle. They have multiplied and increased, until they now estimate the number at a hundred thousand head that are roaming wild over the hills.

The ship being safely moored, I entreated my husband to take me on shore. After much persuasion, he consented. A boat was lowered, in which, after much difficulty, I was placed. This was effected by tying a rope around my waist, and lowering me down the ship's side; then watching an opportunity when the boat was in a right position, to "lower away." This method was of necessity adopted, the sea being so rough, I lacked the courage to leave the ship the usual way. When my feet were placed once more on *terra firma*, I inwardly resolved never again to return on ship-board. We wandered from the shore to the top of a small eminence, from whence, at a little distance, we descried a shanty.

We approached, and, judging from the writing found upon the walls, it had been the resort of sailors thrown upon that inhospitable coast. In it was a sort of stone fire-place, on which the sailors placed some dried heather found in the hut, which, when ignited, threw out a ruddy blaze that sent its cheering beams directly to the heart. On our way to the hut, we noticed several perforations in the earth. One of the sailors, desirous of investigating the origin of these holes, thrust his hand into one of them, but instantly withdrew it with a smothered oath, and an expression evincing acute pain. Immediately, out rushed a penguin, displaying unmistakable symptoms of a fight. Every hole contained a penguin, secreted there for the purpose of incubation. The sailors, of course, exasperated that a brother shipmate should receive such treatment as a reward for his prying curiosity, routed the whole posse of penguins, and a regular hand-to-hand battle ensued; for to the penguins can never be imputed one particle of cowardice, when the call for action is the defence of her eggs or young. Victory was, of course, conceded to the strongest party. But not always does "might make right."

Nothing could be seen in any direction inland but barren hills; yet, cheerless as was the prospect on shore, no entreaty, or even command, of my husband, could induce me to return to that burning ship. Here was a sad dilemma for my husband to be placed in. A sense of duty called him on board; yet he could not leave me on shore all night without a protector. Finally, at the intercession of the mate, who volunteered to take good care of the ship, he reluctantly consented to remain with me, although he spent the greater part of the night watching the ship.

Next morning, as we were about to repair to the boat, — for, upon reflection, I concluded that to be the only way by which the settlement could be reached, — a horseman appeared in the distance, riding at a furious pace directly for us. As he approached, and reined in his jet-black steed in front of our party, I certainly never beheld such a perfect specimen of equestrian grace and manly beauty.

Springing from his horse, he accosted us in a language unintelligible to all except "Old Tom," as he was designated by his shipmates. He proved to be one of a class of men denominated guachos, who are employed in lassoing and bringing in wild cattle. Tom soon acquainted him with every particular concerning us; whereupon he insisted that the capitan's señora should go with him to his ranch, about four miles distant, where every attention would be lavished by his señora to render me comfortable until I could proceed to the settlement.

Tom interpreted the invitation, which, of course, I declined accepting, feeling a reluctancy to go with him alone. Discovering my hesitancy, he endeavored to remove all objections by bestowing several flattering encomiums upon my personal appearance, which were certainly ill-starred, and served only to increase my unwillingness to go with him unattended. It was at length decided that the second mate should accompany me.

Our Spanish friend laughed at the idea of my being afraid to mount his spirited horse, and even objecting to be seated in front of him — the manner in which they often ride with señoritas. He mounted his horse alone; while Mr. Wood and myself walked by his side. My husband returned to the ship. We found it very tiresome travelling over the bogs, with the wind blowing almost a gale. After panting and puffing, and being obliged several times to stop and recover breath, we reached the top of a little eminence; and there, sure enough, was the veritable ranch. It looked so pleasant and home-like about the little cottage, that in vain I endeavored to repress those outgushings of the heart engendered by the sight of objects which recalled vividly to mind home, and all the warm and kindly associations connected therewith.

A lovely little Spanish woman met us at the door, and, after exchanging a few words with her husband, she embraced me affectionately, led me to a pleasant little room looking out upon the bay, and placed a loaf of bread and pitcher of milk on a table by my side. She seemed really grieved because I could not swallow one mouthful. My feelings were fast gaining the ascendency. So much sympathy as she expressed, by her gestures and tender offices, completely won my affections.

I had taken very little food after learning the ship was on fire, and, with feelings all the while wrought to such a state of excitement, the revulsion well-nigh prostrated me. In the meantime, word had reached the settlement that there was a ship in distress outside, and a number of the most popular men of the place had started to render any necessary assistance. Sometime after noon, they reached the Spaniard's house, where we were, and learning of Mr. Wood the particulars, took him into the boat, and, with the exception of three of them, proceeded to meet the ship. It was blowing so hard, they would be compelled to beat the ship up the bay, which would, of course, occupy some time.

Mr. Hamlin, the physician, the surveyor-general, and the clergyman, (the three who remained,) proposed taking the sail-boat belonging to the Spaniard, and take me at once to the colony; and, as their ladies were English, it would be pleasanter than to remain where I was.

Therefore, I bade adieu to my beautiful Spanish friend, and about sundown reached the narrow entrance to the inner harbor. Two large wooden men stand on each side of the entrance, pointing towards the town. Passing through, you find yourself in one of the nicest, land-locked harbors in the world, where ships of the largest tonnage can lie in safety.

The town is built at the base of the hills, which rise gradually from this beautiful basin. How far away from the busy, bustling world seemed this little hamlet! and how quiet and serene, I thought, must pass the lives of those dwelling upon this remote isle! The sun was shedding his last golden rays upon the surrounding hill-tops, before retiring to his hesperian couch. While inanimate nature was welcoming me to this haven of rest, how inexpressibly lonely I felt at heart, surrounded by strangers! No doubt they would extend a friendly greeting; but, oh, how my heart yearned for the warm welcome of some home-friend!

Mr. Hamlin took me to his house, where I was

cordially received by his amiable lady, and nothing was omitted that could in any way contribute to my comfort, or serve to dispel those home-sick feelings which naturally acquired the ascendency. That night, sleep was a stranger to my pillow. I shall ever remember Mrs. Hamlin with feelings of affection. No kind mother could have bathed my aching head more tenderly. Oh, there is a magnetic power in kindness! Kind words are always winning, whether from friend or stranger.

Late in the afternoon, the ship appeared at the entrance. After dropping anchor, my husband called a survey, opened her hatches, and found her to be so badly on fire, they decided to run her ashore, and scuttle her. He selected a spot which happened to be opposite the little grave-yard. Slowly and majestically was she wafted to her place of rest. Never more would she gallantly breast old ocean's wave. With tearful eyes I watched her motions. She had been my home so long, I loved her as such. They cut holes in her side, and sank her in depth of water sufficient to cover the fire. For two days she was enveloped in steam, which precluded all possibility of gaining the deck. After the fire was extinguished, they stopped the holes, and worked the pumps incessantly, without diminishing in the least the depth of water in the ship. She had bilged; her beams and stanchcons were burnt off; and her lower deck had fallen in. She was condemned and sold at auction. It was our intention to go directly home, as soon as an opportunity presented. The isolated situation of the island prevented its being visited often, especially by ships homeward-bound; therefore, our stay there might be indefinitely protracted. There were about four hundred inhabitants in this remote colony, consisting of English, Spanish, and French. The people were under the immediate jurisdiction of a governor, who ruled with despotic power. The governor, clergyman, doctor, governor's secretary, surveyor-general, and lawyer, are appointed by the queen, and receive a salary of four hundred pounds sterling per year, with the exception of the governor, who has eight hundred. These, with their families, also Lloyd's agent, and *the* merchant, constitute the gentry, as they style themselves. The governor lives in princely style. To be seated in his reception-room, one would imagine himself in some English palace. Everything has been transported from England — both house and furniture. All the frame-buildings on the island were brought either from England or the main-land. Those of the poorer class were mere huts, constructed of peat and stone. Peat is also used by them for fuel. Those only who receive a salary can indulge in the luxury of a coal fire.

There is not a tree on the island, with the exception of a few apologies for the same in the governor's garden. They, upon being transplanted into such ungenial soil, had assumed a stinted, sickly appearance.

The governor was a stern, austere-looking personage, greatly to be feared, and seldom loved. One little incident, that came under my own immediate perception, I will relate. It will serve, in a measure, to illustrate his arbitrary propensities. His household consisted of himself, wife, and two sons. The eldest was an imbecile, and so perfectly child-like in his disposition, that he readily won the sympathy of all the inhabitants. The youngest was a wild, head-strong sort of a chap, about fourteen years of age. For him they had employed a young governess, whom they brought with them from England. This young lady they treated more like a menial than as a companion for their children. They looked upon the young instructress as one born to labor and endure, seemingly unconscious that there were as deep fountains of sorrow and love in her heart as there was in those who were fostered in wealth and luxury. One evening, there was a social gathering at the house of Mr. W——; and, of course, Miss T——, being an accomplished and intelligent young person, was present. Upon preparing to leave, early in the evening, (as she was required to be in by nine o'clock,) Mr. W—— proposed to accompany her, as her path lay near the barracks, where were always assembled a drunken, riotous set. Next morning, he received a note from the governor, requesting his immediate presence. Mrs. W—— felt quite alarmed at the thought of her husband incurring the displeasure of his majesty. Upon appearing before this august personage, he received a severe reprimand for so far forgetting his station as a gentleman as to escort home one whom he considered as a dependent upon his bounty, and also assured him, if he was guilty of the like offence again, he should consider him deficient in all that constituted a gentleman.

The governor's wife boasted of being a descendant of the "fair maid of Perth." I have no reason to doubt the tie of consanguinity, although she certainly had not inherited any of the personal attractions of her lovely progenitor..

They were all very kind to us, showing every

respect and attention. Doubtless, I often shocked them with my Yankee provincialisms. Every family of note had magnificent side-boards, stored with the choicest kinds of liquors and cordials. It was considered a breach of etiquette to refuse to partake of the good cheer set before you. What would our American ladies at the present day think of having such an array set before them, when making their accustomed calls? Yet it is universally practised here.

To diminish our expenses, we concluded to go to housekeeping. My husband rented the only vacant building in the place, a miserable, barn-like shanty, for which he paid the exorbitant sum of thirty dollars per month. Thither we moved ourselves: we had little else to move. Nearly every one contributed some article of domestic use. Our larder was supplied with wild-fowl and beef, also a species of fish which are taken from the numerous streams which intersect the country. They are designated trout, but do not in appearance or flavor resemble our own speckled trout, which by epicures are considered such a nice treat. No kind of vegetables could be procured at any price. The inclemency of the weather, even in summer months, precludes the growth of the most hardy kind. Cold storms of hail and sleet are of frequent occurrence in summer. One gentleman, by inclosing a piece of ground with a high peat wall to shelter it from the cold winds, had managed, by dint of great exertion, to raise a few cabbages.

Often, when seated at my window, my attention had been attracted towards a lovely little girl, with soft dark eyes, and long auburn ringlets hanging in rich profusion over her shoulder. She was usually accompanied by a tall, dignified, melancholy-looking individual, who, I afterwards learned, stood in the relation of father. His very countenance, which was seldom irradiated by a smile, bore traces of ineffable sorrow. They would spend hours in sailing around the bay in a fancy yacht, which he kept moored opposite our house. Upon inquiry, I learned that for some time the gossiping and wonder-loving portion of the community had been kept in constant agitation regarding the mystery that surrounded Mr. Montague (for by that name was he known) and his family. He kept himself aloof from all society; and the only servant he kept had never been known to speak an intelligible word to any one. She seemed devotedly attached to her master, and guarded little Myrtie with watchful tenderness. Myrtie came to my door one day, bringing me a basket of nice little fish, and gracefully presented them, saying that she often amused herself by fishing. After that, she became a daily visitor. Daily my interest in that child increased. She was wonderfully endued with intellectual powers for one of her years. One day, she said to me, "Do you know why I brought you those fish? and what brings me every day to see you?" I told her I did not. Said she, "I do so love to look in your face! It makes me feel happy. I always think of some one I loved well, and called mamma. It seems such a long time ago, — so *very* long, — I sometimes think it was a dream. But, since you came here, I can remember more. I can recollect she looked like you; and, when you smile, you look as she used to, when she would kiss me, and call me her little darling. Oh, I remember how I cried when a tall, dark-looking man snatched me from my mamma's arms, — how she looked, as she ran screaming after us!

"I never saw her again. Then old 'Nurse Bell' took care of me. We sailed on the water a long, long time before we came here." Her papa, she said, "was very kind, and she loved him; but she could love him better, if he would talk more about mamma." When she asked him to tell her *all* about her, he would shake his head, look very gloomy, and say, "Your mamma is in heaven." Her father was her only instructor, and she was far advanced in her studies. He also taught her music: she played and sang sweetly. For once I felt inclined to pardon the inquisitive; for they certainly had food for idle speculation. Dear little Myrtie! often have I sighed when thinking of your lonely situation, uncheered by the presence of that guardian angel of childhood — a mother — on whom you could bestow that wealth of affection concentrated in an almost *too* confiding and sensitive heart.

The winter preceding our arrival at the islands had been one of unusual inclemency. Communication with the main-land was entirely cut off before the winter's supply of hay and grain had been procured. In consequence, the cattle suffered incredibly. The snow, for two months, lay upon the ground to the depth of two feet. All the sustenance the cattle could obtain was insufficient to keep off starvation. They were often found dead, thirty and forty in heaps together.

When the English first established this colony, they intended to export hides, tallow, seal-skins, and seal-oil. As yet, they have shipped no tallow Sealing is carried on to a considerable extent.

England's convicts, when banished to the sunny isle of Australia, are not as deserving of the sympathy of the philanthropist as are those old pensioners, to the number of thirty, who, with their families, have been induced, by the promises held out to them, and which they have found, to their sorrow, can never be fulfilled, to leave merry England, for a home on these barren islands.

CHAPTER V.

The feathered tribes are very numerous on these islands of Southern hemisphere. Of penguins, there are four kinds — the king penguin, the macaroni, the jackass, and the rookery. The first of these is much larger than a goose; the other three are smaller, differing in appearance in several particulars. They all walk upright, with their legs projecting from their bodies in the same direction with their tails. When fifty or more of them are seen in file, they appear, at a distance, like a company of soldiers. They carry their heads high, with their wings drooping like two arms. The breast-feathers are delicately white, with a line of black running across the crops. Seen at a distance, they have the appearance of little men, with a white bosom, black neckerchief, and short breeches. Their gait on land, however, is very awkward — rather more so than that of a sailor just returned from a long voyage.

When tamed, the penguin becomes quite tractable. A lady at the isle had domesticated and made quite a pet of a king penguin, which she, however, proposed to relinquish for the sum of thirty dollars. She had taught him to sit at table with her. A sip of coffee he seemed to enjoy with much gusto; and if, perchance, she attempted to raise the cup to her lips before first presenting his majesty with a draught, he would, quick as thought, with a blow from one of his "hands," dash the cup to the floor. He followed her about the house as a child follows its mother; and she assured us he was a great deal of company for her when alone.

Another sea-fowl peculiar to the islands is the upland-goose, which is about the size of our domestic goose. Their plumage is rich and glossy: that of the gander is dazzlingly white. The down is equal to that of the swan. The teal are also found here, and far surpassing in beauty those of this country. Their bills and feet are blue; their wings of a golden green. The ducks are similar to those found in the United States; but the manner of going a-ducking very dissimilar,— no lying in wait half a day before getting a good shot. You might take your gun and shoot them down, and dozens will come to ascertain the cause of the report.

Previous to our arrival, three other vessels had put into the harbor in distress, and had been condemned. The crews of these vessels were constantly out gunning. I would see them often returning over the hills, laden with those beautiful white geese, looking like so many swans. A Dutch captain, whose vessel had been condemned, was very contentedly pursuing the "even tenor of his way," bringing in the game, while "mine frow" was as industriously manufacturing feather beds. Never having heard them say anything about getting away, I presume they are yet at the old vocation.

A moral philosopher and naturalist would be highly interested in contemplating, for days, the operations of a South Sea rookery, observing the order and regularity with which everything is conducted. When a sufficient number of penguins, albatross, etc., are assembled on shore, they proceed to the execution of the grand object for which they left their native element. First, they trace a well-defined parallelogram, of requisite extent to accommodate the whole fraternity,— perhaps from one to four or five acres. One side runs parallel with the water's edge, and is left open for egress and regress. They then commence picking up the stones, and depositing them outside the lines; thus creating quite a little wall on three sides. Within this wall they form a pathway, several feet in width, which would not suffer, in regard to smoothness, compared with any fashionable promenade in our city parks. This path is for the sentinels to patrol at night. They next lay out the whole in little squares, formed by narrow paths which cross each other at right angles. At each intersection of these paths, an albatross constructs her nest; while in the centre of each square is a penguin's nest.

Although the penguin and albatross profess such sincere attachment for one another, they not only form their nests in a different manner, but the penguin will rob her friend's nest, whenever an opportunity presents; being ambitious, I suppose, to produce a large family. The penguin's nest is formed by an excavation in the earth; while that of the albatross is formed by throwing up a mound of earth, eight or ten inches high; on the summit of which she can scrutinize the proceedings of her nearest neighbors and best friends.

The camp of the rookery is in continual motion; penguins passing through the different paths, on their return from aquatic excursions, eager to caress their mates after a temporary absence; while the latter are passing out in quest of refreshment and recreation. At the same time, the air is almost darkened by an innumerable number of albatross hovering over the rookery, continually lighting, and meeting their companions; while others are rising, and shaping their course for the sea. To see these creatures of the ocean so faithfully discharge the duties assigned them by the great Creator; to witness their affectionate re-unions, their numerous acts of tenderness and courtesy to each other, the reflection naturally arises, that, if there was only as much harmony and genuine affection between wedded pairs of the human family, the connubial state would then indeed be "all that we dream of heaven."

We had remained at the islands about a month, when the ship Humayoon, from Dundee, (McKenzie, master,) bound to Valparaiso, laden with coal, tar, and liquors, put into port to procure water and beef. The captain formed an acquaintance with my husband, and, after learning the particulars of our situation, very kindly offered us a passage to Valparaiso; from whence we could, in all probability, arrive home sooner than by remaining where we were. After having procured the necessaries required, I expected the captain would at once proceed on his voyage; but, being perfectly independent, as he was sole owner of the fine ship and cargo, he protracted his stay at the settlement day after day, thereby gratifying the mirth-loving portion of the community by assembling them at different times on ship-board, to join in the merry dance. He had on board several musical instruments, which he was taking out to dispose of; and, being possessed of extraordinary musical talents, the people were perfectly delighted and entranced with specimens of his skill. He had a perfect passion for Scotch airs, which, all conceded, never before sounded half so enlivening. But pleasures, however transporting, unhappily cannot last. No chain, be it of gold, or pearl, or flowers, can bind the stubborn wings of Time, and bid him loiter on his way. On the morning of the 25th of November, he weighed anchor, and turned her bows towards the entrance.

I cast a last, sad, lingering look at the old Nonantum, and bade adieu to kind friends, whom, probably, I should never meet again on the journey of life, although they would be often remembered. During my sojourn at the islands, although I found kind friends, I passed many a gloomy hour. As the season approached which, from time immemorial, in dear old New England, has been observed as a day of thanksgiving and prayer, — a day, of all others, when severed families assemble under the paternal roof, to meet once again the loved friends of their youth, to tread again the paths hallowed by childhood's earliest recollections, — the anniversary of such a day, while in this remote region, crowded my memory with reminiscences of the past, pleasurable, from the associations which they recalled, and painful, from the position which I then occupied.

CHAPTER VI.

Once more I found myself on board a good ship, bounding gayly over the blue waters. Captain

McKenzie possessed, in an eminent degree, the ability of rendering his passengers perfectly at home and happy. His crew were composed entirely of Scotchmen; and, every evening, the echo of their merry Scotch songs were wafted far over the deep sea. Captain McKenzie proposed teaching to me the Spanish language, being a perfect linguist himself. He found me far more tractable in that than in learning to take a glass of his " good Scotch whiskey," as he termed it, to which I had taken a mortal aversion, and for which he entertained a decided preference.

He was a skilful navigator, and, on his voyages around Cape Horn, invariably passed through the Straits of Le Maire, which separate Staten Land from Terra del Fuego, and, by " hugging the land," escape some of the severe blows so prevalent in that region. He having been on several exploring expeditions in those waters, I experienced a degree of security I should not otherwise have felt in approaching so near to huge and jagged rocks, that for ages had reared their frowning heads, as if in defiance of old ocean's roar. We passed the veritable Cape Horn (situated on Hermit Island) in such close proximity, one could distinctly discern the barren soil. While I stood gazing at the conical

BURNING OF THE HUMAYOON.

mount, said the captain, "You have now seen what many an old navigator in these waters never beheld, they keep so far south." I assured him one sight was sufficient for a life-time; that the remembrance of the wildness and grandeur of that ocean scene would never be obliterated from the pages of memory.

That night, it came on to blow tremendously. Next morning, we found ourselves eighty miles from land, and, horror of horrors, the ship on fire! My heart refused to give credence to the startling report, until my eyes beheld it. Our worst fears were too soon confirmed by the flames darting upwards, and igniting the hatch the men were vainly endeavoring to caulk; for fear had paralyzed their faculties. When that burnt and fell in, the flames shot upward almost to the top-mast-head. The combustible nature of the cargo caused the fire to increase with wonderful rapidity. The long-boat was launched, and I was placed therein, with my pet-goat; for I would not leave her behind: the other I had given to Myrtie. After several ineffectual attempts to get at some bread and water, the fire and smoke drove them all in confusion to the boat. They pulled off a short distance, and we gazed in sadness and silence upon what was so recently our happy home, now a burning wreck. The calmness of despair pervaded my whole being: all was comprehended at a glance, — eighty miles from land, and that an inhospitable coast, inhabited only by savages; without bread or water; in an open boat, exposed to the inclemency of Cape Horn weather! People on the land, seated by their pleasant firesides, imagine they can understand our feelings at that time; but it is impossible. Even when danger, in its most appalling form, threatens on the land, there is generally some avenue of escape open. But at sea, with nought but a frail plank between you and a watery grave, — and that so fragile, one dash of those mighty waves might annihilate it, — oh, the horror of such a situation can *never* be conceived!

All at once, the joyful cry of "Sail, ho!" was shouted from our midst; and, far away, I could descry a speck upon the ocean. Nearer and nearer it came, until, when within about a mile of us, she "hove to," and lowered away a boat, which came bounding over the water to our relief. This ship proved to be the Symmetry, of Liverpool, Captain Thompson, bound to Acapulco, and laden with coal. How that word rang in my ears! It seemed to me every ship that floated was coal-laden. We repaired at once on board the Symmetry. Capt. McKenzie requested, as a favor, that Capt. Thompson would "lay by" until the Humayoon was burned down. Now that we could view her from a place of safety, it was a scene to rivet the attention of all beholders. Flying about, at the mercy of the wind and waves, the flames bursting out her sides (the liquor was stowed aft) and stern, the blue flames wreathed and flashed higher and higher. Soon the main and mizen-mast began to totter: they swayed to and fro for about ten minutes, when they fell with a crash over the side. Soon the fore-mast fell; and all that remained of the fine ship Humayoon lay a burning mass upon the water.

Captain Thompson now made sail, and soon the remains of that noble ship which, only twelve days previously, had borne us from our island retreat, was obscured from our view. Her commander dropped a tear to her memory, and retired in silence to the cabin.

Captain Thompson was accompanied by his wife and family. I was pleased at the idea of enjoying for a season, however brief, the society of a female friend. Capt. Thompson had previously informed us that our stay on board the Symmetry must of necessity be prolonged no farther than such a time as he could speak some ship. His inability to accommodate us longer than was actually necessary was owing to a scarcity of provisions, his own ship's crew being then on an allowance. He had been seven months from Liverpool. He had put into Rio on the way, where, on account of severe indisposition, he had remained several weeks. While there, his crew had nearly all deserted him. When ready for sea, he shipped any he could get; and a sorry set he had. Part of them had mutinied, and were confined; and the other half carried the principles of revolt, too apparent to be mistaken, in their dark countenances.

Night had now spread its sable mantle over the world of waters; the bright constellations were reflected in the deep; and the noble ship, with majestic and graceful motion, was cleaving a pathway for herself through the rapidly heaving billows. My thoughts, as my eyes wandered over the waste of waters, were busy with the past and present,— for the future I could only hope. But a few months had intervened since leaving Baltimore; and yet how much intense anxiety, actual suffering, and harrowing suspense, were crowded into that short space! One day on board a burning ship, with no hope of escape; then a port of safety in view; then on board another ship, with every prospect of a speedy termination of our eventful voyage; then, again, assailed by fire, and obliged to seek safety in an open boat, far from land; and then transferred to a place of temporary safety, — for what could we expect but a recurrence of those awful scenes, while on board a coal-laden ship? "What," thought I, "will be the end? Shall I ever be permitted to reach in safety the land of my birth?" I dared not entertain a hope seemingly so fallacious. As time progressed, I was often reminded, by painful contrast, of the fleeting happiness enjoyed on board the Humayoon. *There* a spirit of harmony and love seemed to pervade the whole ship's company. The reverse of this at sea is disagreeable in the extreme; and the truth of this assertion was never more clearly demonstrated than on board the Symmetry. In lieu of heart-stirring songs and happy faces, gloomy frowns, and curses "not loud but deep," met the ear at every turn; anarchy and discord went hand in hand. Daily I scanned the ocean in search of a sail, anticipating a happy change, yet dreading what I most desired; for had not experience taught me that whatever we most earnestly desire, when attained, often proves the source of the keenest misery? At the expiration of thirteen days, the anxiously expected sail appeared. Mentally I prayed it might be an American; for with my own countrymen there exists a congruity of thought and feeling which renders their society more congenial. As she neared us, we perceived, to our great joy, that she was a large American ship. In answer to Captain Thompson's signal, she hove to. He then sent a boat to ascertain if we could be transferred to her. She proved to be the Fanchon, of Newburyport, Captain Lunt, bound to San Francisco, laden with coal, which she took in at Baltimore. We became acquainted with Captain Lunt while at Baltimore. The Nonantum had sailed three weeks in advance of the Fanchon. The Nonantum had gone to her last resting-place; and here, on the broad Pacific, we met the Fanchon, in all her pristine architectural beauty, unharmed, and yet laden with Cumberland coal. Upon Capt. Lunt learning that we were on board the Symmetry, he came with all possible haste in his own boat to convey us to the Fanchon.

In the interim, Captain McKenzie had effected a compromise with Captain Thompson, to the effect that he would sail as near to the port of Valparaiso as would render it safe and feasible for Captain McKenzie and crew to embark in their long-boat, and arrive at their destined port. How well they succeeded, future events will promulgate.

I should judge, the two ships lay about a mile apart. Soon after we welcomed Captain Lunt on board the Symmetry, the heavens became suddenly overcast; and, as appearances betokened a squall, it was thought advisable for me to depart instantly with Captain Lunt; while my husband should collect what effects we had preserved from the Humayoon and my goat, and come in the ship's boat. Thinking and hoping we should reach the Fanchon before the squall struck, they watched us with intense anxiety from the ships. When little more than mid-way between the ships, it came. Drenched with spray, and clinging to my seat, I dared not express my terror other than by looks. "Do not be alarmed," said Capt. Lunt. "There is no danger to be apprehended. We shall soon reach the Fanchon; and, when once on her deck, all trouble and danger will flee away." By such cheering words, he endeavored to divert my thoughts from our by no means enviable situation. My heart almost ceased its pulsations as we bounded over the white-crested billows. How intently were we watched by those on board the Symmetry! When we would disappear from their view in the trough of the sea,

Mrs. Thompson would exclaim, "They are gone! they are lost!" and, when we appeared on the top of some mighty wave, would the fervent exclamation, "Thank God, they are safe!" ascend from every heart. By some mischance or other, in attempting to get alongside, we were swept towards the ship's stern. She was plunging and rolling terribly. "My God, we are under the stern!" was the hasty ejaculation borne to my ears; and there, towering high above us over our frail boat, was the noble ship, threatening instant destruction. It was but momentary. By almost superhuman exertion, the boat's crew succeeded in placing our frail bark beyond the reach of imminent danger; and, as the ship dashed down into the bosom of her native element, we were beyond her reach, but not far enough to escape the tumultuous dashing of the waters, which for an instant caused me to doubt my being in the boat. The second attempt to reach her side was crowned with success. A rope was thrown from the ship, which was caught by those in the boat. It required the united exertions of all to keep the boat from being dashed to pieces against the ship's side. It seemed almost an impossibility for me to ascend the side of the ship unassisted; but so I must go, if I went at all, and that right

TRANSFER FROM THE SHIP SYMMETRY TO THE FANCHON.

speedily. I could scarcely retain an upright position in the boat; and yet, as the ship rolled towards us, my instructions were to jump and catch the man-ropes, and cling hold until she careened the other way, and then to climb the steps as quickly as possible. The water was boiling and surging between the ship and the boat in such a manner as to intimidate a much *larger* female than myself. Captain Lunt was to give the word when to jump; and, when "Now is your time! now is your time!" came thundering in my ears, all my innate fortitude deserted me; I was powerless to move. Captain Lunt, rightly conjecturing that, unless moved by some sudden impulse of resentment, I should never gain the deck, looked and spoke his feelings of disapproval so palpably, (he afterwards assured me it cost him no small effort to conceal his genuine feelings,) that I felt I would make an attempt, "live or die, sink or swim." When next the word was given, it was promptly obeyed. I jumped, caught one of the ropes with both hands, and clung with the tenacity of one whose only hope of preservation depended upon a firm grasp. I was all the time cheered by the cry of "Hold on; you are safe!" In a moment I had clasped the other rope, ascended the steps, and was placed upon deck by the mate.

I could recollect nothing more distinctly, until I found myself in a beautiful cabin, attended by an old man, judging from his silvered locks; yet his fresh and healthy appearance gave evidence that, although "Father Time" had whitened his hair, he had made but few inroads upon a healthy constitution. He was the steward — an old and devoted servant to the captain, in whose employ he had been for seventeen years. He was a native of England. His words of consolation to me were, "God bless your dear little heart!" accompanied by a pat on my shoulder; "may you never be in such a situation again. Lord bless you! The sight of one of my girls in a like situation would well-nigh break my heart." Soon my husband arrived in safety. Captain Lunt made sail, and, long before the shades of evening descended, the Symmetry was scarcely discernible. The Fanchon was far her superior, as regarded sailing qualities and symmetrical proportions. All the symmetry the other could boast of lay in the name. I wished her success, and a safe arrival at her destined port. She had been my home for thirteen days; and, although there were many disagreeable incidents connected with our stay on board, yet she had appeared to render assistance, when our hopes were at the lowest ebb.

Under these considerations, I bade her adieu as an old friend. The cupidity of her captain may be illustrated by the fact of his presenting a bill of one hundred and fifty dollars to my husband, as he was about leaving the ship. There was no alternative but to pay it, situated as we were. For this mean act he was published. The news reached the ear of his employer, who quickly refunded the amount, and also discharged him from his employ. Once again we met the Symmetry, before the termination of this never-to-be-forgotten voyage. When and where, time and future pages will explain.

CHAPTER VII.

OUR home on board the Fanchon was all the most fastidious could desire. Captain Lunt was possessed of all those gentlemanly attributes which are calculated to win the possessor friends, and respect from all with whom he associates. Ever joyous and light-hearted, the salutary effects produced by the exercise of these excellent properties seemed to pervade the hearts of all subject to his control. He also being a judicious disciplinarian, the greatest neatness and order imaginable prevailed throughout the ship. Our fancied security — our sanguine expectations that our troubles from fire at sea were at an end — our hopes of a safe and speedy termination of our voyage — all these heart-cheering feelings were sustained and strengthened by reiterated assurances from Captain Lunt that there was no danger whatever of the Fanchon's burning, she was so well ventilated. In fact, he attributed the destruction of the other ships to want of proper ventilation. Besides, he argued, that if there had been the least probability of its taking fire, it would have done so long ago. We all conceded his arguments were decidedly conclusive; and, for a few days, anxiety, fear, suspense, and all the attendant train of harrowing reflections, were strangers to my bosom. But as frail and fleeting as are all the evanescent joys of earth were my hopes. On the 25th of December, in the evening, as we sat conversing of the day, and the manner in which they were celebrating it at our far distant homes, and vainly wishing that, by another Christmas, our places in the family circle would not be vacant, a puff of air was wafted into the cabin, so strongly impregnated with gas as to render the conviction certain in my mind, that the coal was on fire. I speedily gave utterance to my fears, which met with a responsive "Pshaw! you have inhaled and smelt gas so often, it has become accessory to your very being."

They failed, however, in eradicating from my mind the impression that the coal was on fire. Upon retiring for the night, the thought of being, for the third time, on board a burning ship, so harassed me as to completely banish slumber from my pillow. Next morning, the captain instituted a search throughout the ship, which proved, beyond a doubt in his mind, there could be no fire. We were now about twelve hundred miles from land, with a fair wind, on the direct course for San Francisco.

Things remained in this state for two or three days. I cannot affirm that the minds of *all* were perfectly free from apprehension; yet, as strict watch was kept, and nothing except that disagreeable smell of gas was apparent to confirm my fears, I felt a little more at rest. The third day, as Capt. Lunt was watching one of the large ventilators on deck, he saw something having the appearance of smoke escaping therefrom. He sprang down between decks — there was no appearance of smoke or fire whatever; raised the lower hatch — all appeared as usual. He then ordered the second mate to dig down into the coal, and soon proofs beyond a doubt were too apparent. The coal was so hot, it could not be taken in the hand. The whole body of coal, two or three feet below the surface, was red hot. The same preparations for a life on board a burning ship were again repeated that it had been my fortune twice previously to witness. In this instance, we had not to contend with the elements of wind and water as well as fire; for the ocean, at times, was as smooth and transparent as a glass. For a time, Captain Lunt shaped his course for the Galapagos Islands, what wind there was being favorable to waft us in that direction; and, our distance from the islands and the main-land being nearly equal, he was undecided for some time which port would be our destination. Being within the tropics, the weather was exceedingly pleasant — almost too much so for our benefit.

For several days in succession, it would remain perfectly calm. The nights were beautifully serene; not a cloud, or the slightest film of vapor, appeared on the face of the deep blue canopy of the heavens. The moon, and countless starry host of the firmament, exhibited their lustrous splendor in a perfection of brilliancy unknown to the night-watchers in the humid regions of the Atlantic. The ship would be lying listlessly upon the surface of the unbroken waste of waters, while our minds were constantly agitated between hope and fear, — hope, that each morn, as the golden orb of day appeared rising from old ocean's bosom, that, ere she bid us farewell at eve, some welcome sail would come to the rescue; and fear, as each returning day numbered disappointed hopes, and increased the heat on shipboard, that we were indeed a doomed crew.

At night, signal-lights were kept burning, in the hope of attracting the attention of some vessel which might be passing. For days look-outs were stationed aloft, and more than once were our ears gladdened with the joyful cry of "Sail, ho!" which as often proved a vain illusion. The strained vision and anxious solicitude of those on the look-out caused them to imagine they saw that which they vainly desired to behold.

I was induced, by the entreaties and advice of my husband, seconded by those of Captain Lunt, to adopt gentlemen's apparel. Considering the danger and exposure we might be subjected to, should we be compelled to remain any length of time in the boats, — to which, unless relief arrived from some other source, we should resort to soon, — it was not, everything considered, a bad idea, which might never have been carried into effect had Capt. Lunt been as large in stature as my husband. Accordingly, from the captain's wardrobe was selected a pair of black pants, a green hunting-coat, black satin vest, bosom, and collar worn à la Byron, and a purple velvet smoking-cap. Arrayed in this garb, I was scarcely recognizable by my friends on board. Days came and passed, and yet no relief appeared. Daily, convincing proofs appeared to warn us of the slow but sure destruction of the ship, in the form of gas and smoke, which were escaping through every seam. The beautiful paint-work and gilding of the cabin assumed the darkest hue; everything on board seemed shrouded in the sable habiliments of mourning. Slowly and gradually we neared the land; and, after three weeks of intense suspense and solicitude, the exulting cry of "Land, ho!" was echoed far and near. It was an uninhabited part of the coast of Peru — a small bay, or, rather, indenture made in at this place, called the Bay of Sechura. Into this bay the ship was guided; and, when about two miles from shore, she was brought to an anchor, at about four o'clock, P. M. As soon as the wished-for haven appeared, I hastened to my state-room, and doffed my male attire, supremely happy to exchange what I had so reluctantly adopted, and what each succeeding day of usage rendered still more distasteful. Rest assured, O ye of the opposite sex, that I, for one, will never attempt to appropriate to myself the indispensables, or the love of lordly power which usually accompanies them, but leave *you* in undisputed possession of your rights!

Long before we reached our anchorage, the roaring of the surf, as it dashed upon the lonely beach, sounded like a mournful dirge to our ears. There appeared to be a short stretch of sandy beach, circumscribed by high and jutting rocks. Around us, on either side, were innumerable breakers, threatening destruction as we approached nearer; yet we heeded not our dangerous proximity to sunken rocks, but the noble ship bounded gayly over the waters, unmindful of the destiny awaiting the doomed.

In the distance could be discerned the Andes Mountains, rearing their lofty heads in silent grandeur, and seeming to penetrate the blue dome of the o'er-arching heavens. Immediately upon bringing the ship to an anchor, preparations were made to effect a landing in the boats. Captain Lunt and my husband deposited their nautical instruments and charts, and some few articles of clothing, in a chest which they had rendered as nearly waterproof as possible, and consigned it to one of the boats. We threw overboard all the spare spars upon deck, and everything that would float. We had no provisions or water to take on shore, and had been refreshed with none through the day. There was one pig on board that had left Baltimore in the ship, and one hen. These, together with my pet-goat, the sailors took under their own immediate protection, and succeeded in landing them on the beach. The pig, in the height of his terror, beat an instantaneous retreat into one of the numerous caves, or recesses, situated at the base of perpendicular cliffs, which rose nearly two hundred feet, and presented an effectual barrier to any attempt that might be made to scale them. I recollect distinctly my sensations on leaving the ship in a boat; how intently I watched the foaming surf we were fast approaching, and which had already engulfed the boat in advance; then an indistinct recollection of roaring and splashing of water, — of voices heard above the din of all, giving directions, — of being dragged, minus bonnet and shawl, through the surf

BURNING OF THE FANCION ON THE COAST OF PERU.

upon the sandy beach. Of my very unceremonious introduction within the precincts of the province of Peru, I have no very pleasing recollections. After removing everything off the ship's deck, they ran her still nearer in, and scuttled her; but the fire had made such progress, it was impossible to save her. In two hours after we left her deck, she burst out into a sheet of flame. The fire caught to the sails, which were spread to the breeze, and she was a sheet of fire to the mast-heads. Here, in this lonely bay, lay the fine ship Fanchon, and burnt to the water's edge. Nothing could exceed the almost awful profoundness of the solitude by which we were surrounded — a silence broken only by the roaring and crackling of the flames, as they wreathed and shot far upward, illuminating the midnight darkness, and casting the reflection of their fiery glare far out over the lonely deep, — and the deep roar of the eternally restless waves, as they dashed in rapid succession upon the beach at our feet. It is quite impossible to convey by language an adequate conception of the solemn magnificence of this midnight scene. The burning ship in the foreground, the light from which revealed the sublime altitude of the mountains in the background, whose barren heads seemed to pierce the sky, every object distinctly daguerreotyped; the rocks on either hand, laved for ages by the white sea-foam; the bald and inaccessible cliffs in close proximity, in the rear; and twenty-six human beings (myself numbering the only female) standing upon the narrow beach, viewing silently the work of destruction, rapidly progressing, which deprived us of a home, and the necessary sustenance required to support life, — only a skilful artist, with his pencil and brush, could do justice to the picture here drawn. By three o'clock that night, nought remained to mark the spot — where, a few hours previous, lay the gallant ship — but a smoking hulk.

I sank into an unquiet slumber superinduced by exhaustion, fairly cried myself to sleep, and rested my weary limbs upon a couch of beach-sand. Next morning, we discovered several rafts (or, as they are there denominated, balsas) coming into the bay. They were covered with Indians — a sort of mongrel race, who live principally upon their balsas, scarcely ever visiting the shore except to procure water and potatoes. They subsist mostly upon raw fish. They speak the Spanish language. They anchored their crafts outside the surf, then dove into the water, and swam to the shore. They were nearly in a state of nudity. Their demeanor was entirely pacific. They advanced towards us with hands extended, in token of friendship. They had been attracted to the spot by the light from the burning ship, and had assembled in considerable numbers, doubtless in the hope of obtaining pillage, as they rather demurred in rendering any assistance, unless stimulated by a promise of compensation. For "mucha pesos," they agreed to furnish us with water and sweet potatoes while we remained upon the beach. They peremptorily refused to take us to Payta,—the nearest settlement,—which was fifty miles distant,—thinking, doubtless, it would be a more profitable speculation for them to protract our stay upon the beach, until, at least, the "pesos" were all gone. I was constrained to offer my pet-goat to them, in exchange for water: she had long since ceased to furnish milk. Poor thing! after having encountered so many fiery trials, she was but a wreck of her former self. Much as I regretted to part with her, I felt it to be a duty I owed her, for past favors received, to mitigate her woes as far as it lay in my power. With a last, sad, lingering look at her mistress, and a despairing farewell bleat, she was dragged away. The natives informed us we were fifteen leagues from any fresh water; thereby giving us to understand that we were very dependent mortals. They then departed, promising to come on the morrow with a fresh supply. Their balsas are constructed of very buoyant, porous logs, bound together in the form of a raft; then another layer, transverse the former. In the centre, it is raised still higher.

CHAPTER VIII.

Here indeed was a new phase of existence, gloomy enough in anticipation, yet far preferable to the dangerous scenes in which it had heretofore been my fortune to participate. The sailors pitched four small tents; two for themselves, and two for the officers. These served for a shelter at night; but, during the day, when the sun shone with an almost scorching fervency of heat, unmitigated by a single cloud on the face of the sky, it was almost impossible to remain in them. To augment our troubles, the fleas were so numerous and so bloodthirsty, that for a few days I was in perpetual motion. When once they made a lodgment in our clothing, it was useless to attempt to exterminate them; and *they* never capitulate. At night, upon retiring, our only preparation was to spread a blanket upon the sand, and lie down upon it. In the morning, we would find ourselves almost imbedded in the loose beach-sand; for, upon the dry part of the beach, it was quite deep. I would rise, and shake my head to dislodge the quantity of sand there collected. My hair was hanging unconfined over my shoulders, having lost comb, hair-pins, and bonnet. I would walk down to the shore of the Pacific, — an ample wash-bowl, certainly, — and perform my ablutions, dispensing, of necessity, with all the modern appurtenances of a lady's toilet.

Captain Lunt proposed to send to the American Consul at Payta for assistance to remove us from the beach. His mate, Mr. McCrelles, of Belfast, Maine, volunteered to go, accompanied by four of the sailors. The next day after our arrival there, they embarked on their voyage to obtain the relief we so much needed. Their directions were, to keep close in shore; and, with God's blessing, they would arrive at Payta, and assistance would reach us at the expiration of a week. We watched the little boat until she looked like a speck upon the water; and, with many an unuttered prayer for her safe arrival, we turned our thoughts landward,

—I to amuse myself by selecting the most beautiful shells I could find: they were very numerous among the rocks at each extremity of the beach. I was never lonely: I found companions in my own thoughts; and they were oftentimes pleasanter than the gayer ones of the world would have been, for they whispered of home and loved friends.

There was the skeleton of a whale perfect, and entirely exposed. How long the remains of this huge aquatic monster had been bleaching under the scorching rays of that tropical sun, we had no means of ascertaining.

The Indians faithfully kept their promise, and each succeeding day they visited us with a plentiful supply of water and potatoes; the bill of fare varied occasionally by the introduction of some very offensive fowl, which they positively asserted were "esta bueno." An amusement in which I often indulged was to chase innumerable crabs, with which the beach was literally covered in the mornings. They would, upon the first intimation of pursuit, disappear instantly into their holes in the hard sand. By remaining perfectly quiet for some time, they would again assemble in numbers, which the least movement on my part would again put to flight. They would make greater progress running sideways than I could any way; therefore, I never caught one.

The pig remained secreted in his cavernous retreat, which no entreaties on our part could induce him to vacate. Not until driven to the last extremity by the pangs of hunger, did he venture to reconnoitre from the aperture. After viewing his companions in distress for a little time, he gained sufficient courage to eat potatoes from my hand. After that, he became quite domesticated, and, with the hen, used to share the sailors' tent with them at nights.

During this time, I was unconsciously assuming the dark and swarthy hue of the native women, from being constantly exposed to the scorching glare of a tropical sun. My habiliments, too, were becoming exceedingly soiled, from constant use both by night and day.

The love and spirit of adventure had, from earliest infancy, been strongly implanted in my nature; and, during this voyage, certainly, this predilection for thrilling adventure had been amply gratified. Yet, had not the fiery ordeal through which it had pleased the God of love to bring me been for good, it would have been averted.

A week had now elapsed since the departure of

the boat. Intently we scanned the ocean, in the hope of descrying the anxiously expected sail. Nights, at the hour of twilight, I would seat myself upon the rocks to indulge in the reveries which that most fitting hour for reflection usually calls up. The mind feels a soothing influence as the light of day fades gradually from sight. At such times memory is busy with the past — the distant home, the loved friends there assembled. I often wandered in this way through the spirit-land of old times. One night I was startled by the exultant cry of "A sail! a sail!" Being fearful lest some casualty had befallen the boat, and she had never reached Payta, Captain Lunt deemed it advisable to make signals, in the hope of attracting attention. She kept on her way, apparently unmindful of the signals which she could not but have seen, as the captain had sent up a rocket, which he had preserved in the water-proof chest. Darkness now hid her from our view; and we sat down, wondering that no answering signal had been displayed to our call for succor.

We repaired to our tent with our minds illy reconciled to passing another night victims to the insatiable fleas, whose cry still was, Blood, blood. All at once we heard the clanking of chains letting go an anchor. All rushed out, and there lay a dark object in the offing. Soon we heard the splash of oars; and in a short time Mr. McCrellis, his countenance beaming with smiles, stood in our midst. He was accompanied by Captain Hillman, originally of New Bedford. His bark had been chartered by the American consul to come to our rescue. The next morning we bade farewell to rocks, and sand, and fleas, and repaired on board the bark, where, for the first time since leaving the Fanchon, I caught a glimpse of my sun-burned, swarthy countenance. The poisonous bite of the fleas had contributed their share towards imparting to my skin the appearance of a person suffering from measles, small-pox, and erysipelas combined.

CHAPTER IX.

As you enter the harbor of Payta from sea, the town presents a most uninviting appearance. It is built at the base of sand hills. The houses have the appearance of mud huts; the roofs covered with tile. Upon a nearer approach, not a green thing can be discovered except the balconies of some of the finer houses. The consul, tired, as he said, of eternally seeing sand hills and sand-colored dwellings, had relieved the monotony of the scene by substituting green paint wherever an opportunity presented. At this time the town numbered about four thousand inhabitants. They came to an anchor some distance from the shore, and were soon surrounded by boats. The English, French, and American consuls came on board, each equally desirous of giving us a home, and contributing in any way to render our stay with them as pleasant as possible. We repaired to the house of the American consul — Mr. Ruden, of New York, who has a mercantile house established there. This house is very spacious, constructed upon the Spanish plan of architecture, and constructed wholly after the manner of South American houses. The whole front of the lower part is appropriated to business.

A wide and pleasant balcony surrounds the entire house at the second story. Large windows, and still larger doors, open upon this balcony, and render it an airy and delightful residence. From this balcony you have a fine view of the harbor, dotted with ships of almost every nation. In addition — and not a very pleasant auxiliary, to be sure — are multitudes of natives constantly sea-bathing, and frolicking in the water. I often wondered if some of them were not really amphibious. Mr. Ruden's household consisted of himself and four gentlemen belonging to the firm. All his servants were male natives, and he employed quite a number, with a major domo to superintend them. Upon entering the spacious parlor, my attention was attracted to the portrait of a lady with such a pleasant expression of countenance that I hoped the original was not far distant. In this, however, I was disappointed. It was a portrait of Mr. Ruden's mother, a resident of New York city. Mr. Ruden was a bachelor; thus again was I deprived of female companionship. Eighteen years of his life had been passed in South America, where he had amassed quite a fortune.

I often availed myself of the use of Mr. Ruden's library. In this room was suspended a hempen hammock, in which I enjoyed many a delightful siesta. The bedsteads were all of polished brass, and very beautifully curtained with bright-colored satin. Some of them cost as high as one thousand dollars. The pillow-slips and counterpanes were solid embroidery, executed by the delicate hands of the lovely Spanish señoritas. They were placed on the beds over a lining of pink or blue cambric, thereby displaying to great advantage the fine needle-work. Even the toilet-towels were embroidered at each end a quarter of a yard in depth, and then fringed. We breakfasted at ten o'clock, and dined at five, P. M. At nine, P. M., a servant would bring us a most excellent cup of tea, which we generally enjoyed seated upon the balcony. Through the day we were regaled with all the delicious fruits indigenous to a tropical clime, among which were several kinds I had never before tasted — the palta and cherrymoyer. The first-named is shaped something like cucumber, and is eaten with pepper and salt. The flavor of the cherrymoyer is perfectly delicious. This fruit is about the size of the largest kind of Baldwin apple, and very pulpous. The fruit, together with the water, and all the vegetables consumed in Payta, and all with which the shipping is supplied, is transported across a desert of sixteen miles in width, upon mules' backs, from a town called Piura — a perfect garden of Eden, through which flows a pellucid river. When the ladies of Payta visit Piura to refresh themselves with a sight of the beautiful in nature, they are transported in a palanquin, which is rested upon the shoulders of natives. On the desert there is not a tree or shrub to mark one's course. It is deep sand, from which footprints are quickly erased. A pocket-compass is indispensable in crossing.

There was a church near to Mr. Ruden's house, which I often frequented — at the matin hour, and again at vespers — to get a view of the lovely brunettes, who, with heads uncovered, were kneeling in every direction, upon soft mats brought every day by a servant, following in close proximity to the señora or señorita. I admire their style of beauty. The clear olive complexion; the soul and sympathy which beam from their dark, lustrous eyes; their long, black, glossy hair; their natural ease, grace, and warmth of manner; the lip so full of sentiment and love, that, if the eyes were closed, the face would retain its exquisite expression; their vivacity of manner in conversation — *all* unite to form a lovely and fascinating woman.

The walls of the churches are hung with coarse paintings, and engravings of the saints, etc., etc. The chancel is decorated with numerous images and symbolic ornaments used by the priests in their worship. Gold paper and tinsel in barbaric taste are plastered without stint upon nearly every object that meets the eye. When, on festive occasions, the church is lighted, it presents a very glittering appearance. The tastes and predilections of the priests are totally unlike what one would suppose their sacred offices would instigate. I have seen a priest leave the church, walk directly to his house, take two fighting-cocks, one under each arm, and repair to the scene of cock-fighting, and there spend hours in betting.

While at Payta, the United States sloop-of-war Vincennes, Commander Hudson, arrived in port. The officers frequently dined with Mr. Ruden. By invitation of Captain Hudson, we all dined on board the Vincennes. We were welcomed alongside by a salute of twenty-one guns — a compliment usually conferred upon a consul when he visits ships of the line. We spent the afternoon most agreeably; and the refined hospitality, courteous manners, intelligent and interesting conversation of our host, made us regret the rapidly fleeing moments. It was a beautiful moonlight eve when we left the Vincennes in the captain's barge, rowed by those men-of-war sailors, dressed with such uniform neatness. Not a ripple disturbed the placid and glossy surface of the water. At night so pure is the atmosphere, that the moon gives a light sufficiently powerful for the purposes of the reader or student who has good eyesight. There is no necessity of burning the "midnight oil;" nature here lights the lamp for the bookworm. So phosphorescent is the water, that every dip of the oars is followed by a stream of light resembling fire. When we were at Payta, we were informed that no rain had fallen during the preceding seven years. We met there a friend from whom we had parted on the broad Pacific, never expecting to meet again — Captain McKenzie. Yes! the pleasant Scotch captain we left on board the Symmetry. Captain Thompson had faithfully fulfilled the stipulation to leave them near the port of Valparaiso. From thence he had taken passage in an English steamer bound to Panama, and from there he would cross the isthmus, proceed to New York, and from there to England. The steamer touched at Payta to remain an hour, and Captain McKenzie stepped on shore to have a view of the town. Nearly the first persons he saw were Captain Lunt and my husband. When he parted from us last, we were bound to San Francisco. Judge, then, of his astonishment at meeting them there. He knew at once some unforeseen calamity had driven them from their course. From previous events his thoughts naturally reverted to fire; and his first exclamation was, "My God! you have been burnt out again!" Too true. All was then explained. There they met, at a port neither of them intended to visit — the three captains who had lost their ships by fire. He paid me a passing visit at the house, then departed on his way to his distant home, to gladden the anxious hearts of wife and children. I have never seen or heard from him since. But, whenever my thoughts revert to him, the recollection is always flavored with old Scotch whiskey.

The bark Carbargo, Captain Barstow, was loading at Payta for Panama. The captain was a native of Pembroke, Mass., and, being acquainted with our friends at home, felt quite an interest in our welfare. He very kindly offered to give us a passage to Panama. Upon his assuring me he had not a cargo of coal, but mules, sheep, and fowl instead, I felt I might safely trust myself once more on board another vessel. It was a lovely day we bade good-bye to Mr. Rudén and other friends, with whom we had passed many pleasant hours during a four weeks' sojourn at Payta. I had changed somewhat in my personal appearance since first I beheld those everlasting sand-hills.

My wardrobe, too, had been replenished. I was really a gainer by my temporary stay at Payta, and departed with a lighter heart. Hope seemed to whisper of a cloudless to-morrow. How wisely ordered, how characteristic of our natures, to hope on, hope ever! When Hope deserts her throne, we are, indeed, like a lost mariner without chart or compass.

Here we are again on ship-board; and I have no better business, all these long summer days, than to watch those thirty large mules, ranged along the deck, fifteen on a side, their heads facing the vessel's rail, with just a path between the rows. They were the finest-looking mules I ever saw. The South American mule is larger, as a general thing, than the Mexican mule. The captain anticipated realizing a handsome sum for them. They were in excellent order, and were blessed with such nice long tails, which is considered quite an acquisition. One morning early, I heard such a loud talking on deck, and in no very pleasant tones either, I conjectured something awful had happened. I soon ascertained the cause of the clamor. One of the mules had broken his fastening in the night, and, not being discovered, had the extreme audacity to deprive nearly all his brother mules of their dearly prized appendages, eating the hair square off, up to the fleshy part of their tail. It appears they invariably practise this habit whenever they can get them in a position where they can make no resistance. The sheep were between decks. The heat must have been almost insupportable. They would gather round the wind-sail with their noses up, panting terribly. It was not an agreeable cargo; yet I had no fears of spontaneous combustion, although I afterwards learned there was coal in for ballast.

CHAPTER X.

Upon arriving in the harbor of Panama, we came to an anchor about two miles from the city. Ships scarcely ever go nearer on account of rocks. It is not a very good harbor for vessels to lie in with safety, it is so open. At anchor close by us was the ship Marianna, of San Francisco, Captain Rossiter. He recognized my husband as an old acquaintance, invited us on board his ship, where he was enjoying the society of his wife and an interesting little child. Captain Rossiter informed us he was going to take his ship down to Taboga, an island which lies about ten miles from Panama. The P. M. S. S. Co. have a depot there. All the steamers, when in port, lie there. The shipping frequent this place to get a supply of water, which gushes in clear rivulets down the sides of the mountains. A little steamer plies constantly between Taboga and Panama for the accommodation of passengers, who are constantly flocking from the miasma-infected city of Panama, to inhale the health-breathing zephyrs of this island retreat. The shore is very bold. Ships of the largest tonnage lie within a stone's throw of the shore. Nearly all the washing is carried from the city, and here cleansed in the running streams by the native women, and spread upon the bushes to dry. At this time there were three hotels there, and quite a number of native populace. Since the time I allude to, they have been visited by a destructive fire. It has been rebuilt, however. We spent one happy week here. Daily Mrs. Rossiter and myself wandered up and down the mountain's side, protected from the sun's rays by the umbrageous foliage which formed a complete net-work above our heads. Here grew the cocoa-nut and pine-apple. The monkeys chattered and swung from branch to branch above our heads. The parrot and paroquet screamed at us from their leafy habitations. Birds of beautiful plumage were carolling their sweetest notes, giving to these sylvan mountain-slopes a truly vivifying appearance. Here, thought I, in company with loved ones, could I dream away a happy existence. The impersonations of romance and solitude could scarcely find a more congenial abode than this beautiful and sequestered isle. At the expiration of this memory-treasured week, which was, indeed, an oasis in the waste over which I had been wafted, we returned to an anchor at Panama. That night I was suddenly and severely attacked with what was conceded to be, by all, Panama fever of the most malignant kind. The next day I was carried on shore, through the city, to a house outside the city gates, owned by a gentleman from New Orleans. For the use of one furnished room and board, the sum of forty dollars per week was required. It was a large, barn-like dwelling. Nearly all the rooms were rented to Spaniards. The partitions which divided the house into apartments only extended to a height sufficient to conceal the occupants from one another, without in the least obviating the noise and disturbance naturally occurring from so many living under one roof. Even this tenement, rough as it was, far exceeded, in point of cleanliness and healthy location, the crowded, and at that time filthy, hotels of the city. Ours was a corner room in the second story, fronting the street. Large doors, very much resembling barn-doors, opened from two sides of the room upon a balcony, that indispensable appendage to all the dwellings situated in tropical climes. Every breath of air which fanned my burning brow seemed wafted from a heated furnace. For days I lay a victim to that consuming fever, part of the time in blissful unconsciousness. I say blissful, because my thoughts wandered to my distant home, and I was relieved, for the time being, from the agonizing thoughts that in intervals of reason obtruded themselves upon me. I was attended by no physician. Captain Rossiter administered dose after dose of calomel, until my system was completely prostrated. Well was it for me that my knowledge of the Spanish language was so limited; otherwise I might have been shocked by the language of some of the inmates of the house. Every footfall, every loud word, echoed and reverberated through that hollow building, sending, at each recurrence, a pang of agony through my burning brain. Fear, too, would assert her sway when left alone, as I oftentimes was. For nearly two weeks the fever raged incessantly; after which time, I gradually convalesced.

When raised by pillows in my bed, I had a view of the street leading to the rear gates of the city, and day after day could I see the silent dead borne to their last resting-place. At that time, Panama was crowded with Americans waiting to be conveyed to the gold-studded placers of California. Alas! many of the number never reached the goal they so ardently desired, and for which they had sacrificed their own happiness, and that of those dearer to them than aught else except gold, the yellow dust of temptation. Truly it may be said to be "the root of all evil," when it allures thousands from their peaceful homes, to meet an untimely death. Reflections such as these had a decided tendency to depress still more my already despondent heart. My recovery, at times, was considered doubtful. It was too sickly to entertain the idea of remaining there longer than was absolutely necessary. I was too weak to attempt to cross the Isthmus; therefore, all hope of returning home was abandoned.

It was decided to take passage at once for San

Francisco. We remained one month at Panama. During the last two or three days of our stay, I walked a short distance each day. One of our walks we extended as far as the burying-ground. What a shunned and desolate spot was that American burial-ground at Panama, — a mere necessary receptacle of lifeless flesh and crumbling bones, — not even a stone raised to mark the last resting-place of the many loved friends who had breathed their last sigh in a strange land, and by strangers been consigned to mother earth! A little piece of board was sometimes reared, with the name, age, and place of residence, marked thereon; but often this little mark of respect and affection had been displaced by mules, numbers of which are constantly grazing among the graves. No inclosure protects these often nameless mounds; straggling bushes struggle with rank and choking weeds that overtop them. The whole place bears a deserted, forsaken aspect — untrodden by the feet of memory and love. It is within sight of the bay, whose waters, as they eternally dash against the shore, seem to be chanting a requiem for the departed. The evening before we left Panama, our attention was attracted by what we conceived to be a torch-light procession, issuing from the city gate. Upon a nearer approach, it proved to be a funeral cortege. First came several horsemen bearing torches; these were followed by a band of music, playing very lively, heart-stirring strains; then came an open bier, carried by natives, upon which was borne the lifeless remains of a sweet little cherub, a lovely Spanish child — lovely even in death. It seemed to be in a sitting posture. In each hand was placed a wax candle; wreaths of flowers entwined its angelic brow, and were strewn in rich profusion upon the bier. Innumerable wax tapers were inserted around the outer edge of the bier, which shed an ethereal halo upon the little form of clay, which had so recently been the pride and joy of fond parents. Then followed another company of equestrians and pedestrians. It had the appearance of some joyous festive scene rather than a funeral procession. And, truly,

> "Why should we mourn for the child early called
> From the sin and the suffering of this darkened world?
> Though ties of affection may early be riven,
> Why wish back on earth the dear loved one in heaven?"

Oh, how I suffered, while at Panama, for a draught of cold water, to allay that feverish, burning thirst which seemed to be consuming the very life-blood in my veins! By the time they could get the clear, cool water from the gurgling rivulets of Taboga to Panama, it would be tepid, and I would turn from it in disgust. Often, in my hours of delirium, would I fancy myself at home, travelling again the little school path. I would arrive at the running brook which wandered through green meadows, and was spanned by a rustic bridge, over which, for twelve happy years, our little feet had skipped each day, on the way to and from school. Then I would fancy myself leaning far over the grassy brink — so far, I could touch my lips to the transparent surface, and imbibe draught after draught of the sparkling liquid. Pleasing hallucination! too quickly dispelled by returning reason. In my lucid moments, I was ever thinking of the old well at home, and wishing for *one* drink from the " moss-covered bucket." I felt it would save my life, when all else should prove abortive. One who has never been prostrated by fever in a burning tropical clime, when it was utterly impossible to obtain ice or cool water, can scarcely conceive of the torture and agony endured. Every breath of air is a simoom to the sufferer. My principal sustenance was the banana and plantain.

We took passage in the steamer Republic for San Francisco. The price of our tickets at that time were six hundred dollars. The Republic was commanded by Captain William Hudson, a son of the commander of the sloop-of-war Vincennes. He was a lieutenant in the navy, but was then enjoying a furlough of four years, which he improved by taking charge of the Republic.

I saw nothing of the city of Panama except what met the eye in passing through its narrow streets, — more properly, lanes, — bounded on either side by high, prison-looking buildings, with iron bars in lieu of window-sashes. Plenty of naked natives, all eager to carry us on board in their bungoes (boats), — a noisy, wrangling set they were, — assembled there upon the beach. Immediately upon reaching the steamer, I repaired to my state-room, and, in an exhausted state, was assisted into my berth. I remained in this situation through all the hurry and bustle incident to the departure of an ocean steamer, but then was fated to be disturbed in a manner I little dreamed of. A lady came to the state-room, and very unceremoniously demanded my berth, saying her ticket, which she had purchased in New York, called for it. Here was a dilemma! The ticket calling for that berth had been sold twice. Captain Hudson was called to the rescue. He decided I should not be removed. He had previously been informed of the series of accidents that had befallen us on our eventful voyage, and declared, laughingly, that, unless routed by fire, I should not be molested. He offered to provide the lady from New York with another room; which she obstinately refused to occupy, vehemently averring that she would lie upon the cabin-floor, and prosecute the company for practising such duplicity. This threat she put in execution upon her arrival at San Francisco, and received compensation to the amount of several thousand dollars.

Upon getting out to sea, my recovery was visibly accelerated by the invigorating sea-breezes and cheerful companionship of our fellow-voyagers. I made many pleasant acquaintances, and formed friendships which have endured to the present, — not the fashionable friendship of an hour, which dishonor the name, but attachments that have stood the test of adversity and misfortunes. The steamer Republic had on board four hundred passengers. Thirty out of this number were ladies, — the largest number which, at that time, had been taken on board any one steamer to San Francisco. There were but very few of them accompanied by their husbands; the remainder were going to meet their liege lords, from whom they had been separated, some two years and longer. It was very amusing to listen to the various conjectures advanced as to the probability of their being recognizable, after being for so long a time strangers to the hair-clipping propensity of the razor. In those early days of California hair-producing memory, when the passion for gold-hunting completely absorbed all other faculties, but very little time or attention was expended upon their persons.

The steamer put into Acapulco to coal up. The harbor reminded me somewhat of Port Stanley, although it is not quite so completely land-locked. The natives swam off to the ship in numbers; while the passengers amused themselves by throwing over pieces of money, which, as it was sinking, they dove after, and obtained with surprising dexterity. They appeared again upon the surface, in an incredibly short space of time, with their dark countenances illumined by a grin, illustrative of much delight, holding high the hand, and displaying the rescued coin. Then they would deposit it quickly in their mouths, and be in readiness for another dive. The most successful one was easily detected by his protuberant cheeks. To deceive, one of the passengers threw over a button. Upon discovering the deception practised, no enticement could afterwards induce them to dive after what fell from his hand. Their discriminating powers must be very acute to recollect the countenance of that gentleman among so many strange faces. We remained nearly one day at Acapulco, which most of the passengers improved by wandering through the town and its suburbs.

Not having recovered my health sufficiently to endure a tiresome tramp, I only saw that part of the town in immediate proximity to the harbor. I was very favorably impressed, however. It was the cleanest, neatest, most cheerful-looking Spanish town I had ever beheld. Shops of every description met the eye, almost bewildering the senses with the multifarious display. The cafés at every corner sent out a cheering welcome to the olfactory organ; the bazaar was thronged with people displaying fruit in all its stages, sufficient, if partaken of, to prostrate the whole ship's company; and the incomprehensible jargon of the venders reminding one of (as some express it) "bedlam let loose." Sometimes one feels half inclined to purchase, if for nought else than to win one of those irresistible smiles from the señorita in attendance.

Upon entering the harbor, the first thing that met my eye was the ship Symmetry, which came to our deliverance off Cape Horn. She had, after a tedious voyage, reached her destination. Capt. Thompson recognized us from the deck of the Symmetry, and came on board to see me. He informed me his crew were all in the lock-up, and there he intended to keep them, to ensure better behavior in future. He looked really care-worn, from continued and incessant trials. I pitied him more than I liked him. We wondered at his coming to see us. I never saw him more.

Soon we were again steaming our way along the coast to San Francisco. One night, we were all startled from our slumbers by the quick ring of the fire-bell, and the wild shout of "Fire! fire!" ringing loud and clear from the deck. Oh, what a rushing and screaming with the ladies! what terrified looks, as they crowded and pushed one another up the stairs, in mad haste to gain the deck! It was a scene of terrible confusion; in the midst of which I stopped to put on shoes and stockings. I say not this to boast of more self-possession or calmness in moments of peril than naturally belongs to the sex; but, having been so often subjected to the fiery ordeal during that eventful year, I had learned to expect it as a matter of course, and was not so startled or unprepared by the recurrence of such an event as those more favored, who had recently left pleasant homes, and had encountered nought but sunshine. It appeared one of the waiters had gone to the engineer's room (which was upon deck), to draw alcohol from a cask. It ignited by a spark from the lamp; the cask exploded, and set fire to the room. The boy rushed out in terror, rang the bell, and cried "Fire!" at the top of his voice. One of the engineers, who was in bed at the time, was severely burned. The greatest confusion prevailed for awhile, after the passengers gained the deck *en masse*. Some sprang to the boats, attempting to cut away the lashings, and were only deterred from committing this dastardly act through fear of having a bullet put through their heads. Several amusing and ludicrous incidents transpired also. One man took his umbrella in one hand, and carpet-bag in the other, and was caught in the act of jumping overboard. A Jew, who had on board goods to the amount of several thousand dollars, was offering them to any one for a bid of three hundred dollars, and cash down. The old adage, "the ruling passion strong in death," was here verified.

It was pronounced at once by all the ladies, that I must be the "Jonah;" and really I began to think there might be some truth in the assertion.

CHAPTER XI.

The last of April, 1851, after an eventful and tedious voyage, we approached the entrance to the harbor of San Francisco, appropriately denominated the "Golden Gate." The entrance is about a mile and a half in breadth. The waters of the bay appear to have opened for themselves a passage through the elevated ridge of hills next to the shore of the Pacific, which rise abruptly on either side of the opening. There is always depth of water sufficient to admit ships of the largest size; and so completely land-locked and protected from the winds is the harbor, that vessels can ride at anchor in perfect safety, in all kinds of weather. The harbor is sufficient to accommodate all the navies in the world. As the emigrant approaches California from the ocean, Monte Diabolo is the first land by which the eye is greeted. It is situated in Contra Costa county, sixty or seventy miles distant from Sacramento, in a south-westerly direction. According to the best information obtained, the altitude of this mountain is about five thousand feet above the level of the sea. It stands at the north-western termination of the inner coast range, disjointed and isolated, and, like most of its bleak and sterile companions, is rent· by deep fissures and yawning chasms, which give it the appearance rather of a cluster of small mountains than one ponderous pile. But little is yet known of the geological history of Monte Diabolo, or the "Mountain of the Devil." San Francisco is situated on the south side of the entrance, fronting on the bay, about six miles from the ocean. The bay, from the city of San Francisco due east, is about twelve miles in breadth. A range of high hills bounds the view on the opposite side. Between them and the shore is a broad and fertile plain, called the Contra Costa. Quite a little village had sprung up there, on the shore of the bay, when I last saw the place, called Oakland.

Yerba Buena (sweet herb) is an island in the bay, and almost directly fronting the city of San Francisco, a mile or so distant. There are several small islands in the bay. Opposite San Francisco, on the north side of the bay, is a place called Sausolito, where, at an early period in the history of San Francisco, vessels repaired, preparatory to sailing, to take in their water. Now, water-boats are plying between Sausolito and the city, affording ample remuneration for the toil. On the right-hand side of the bay, as you are approaching the city, is situated the Presidio of San Francisco. It consists of several blocks of adobe buildings, covered with tiles. The walls of most of the buildings are crumbling for the want of care in protecting them from annual rains.

At a distance of a mile and a half from the entrance to the bay, are the remains of an old fort. It is fast going to decay, daily threatening a complete ruin. The guns are dismounted, and some of them are half decomposed from exposure to the weather. When I passed through the Golden Gate for the last time, there was in process of erection a fortification on one of the bluffs commanding the entrance. Outside, lay the wreck of the clipper-ship Golden Fleece; the ceaseless motion of the waves chanting a requiem over her remains.

At San Francisco, during the summer and autumnal months, the wind blows directly from the ocean, rendering the temperature cool enough in the afternoon for woollen clothing, in midsummer. The mornings are usually calm and pleasantly warm. About sunset, the wind dies away, and the nights are comparatively calm. In winter months, the wind blows in soft, balmy breezes from the south-east; the thermometer rarely sinking below 50 deg.

When the winds blow from the ocean, it never rains. When they blow from the land it is lowery, and resembles that of the month of May, in the same latitude on the Atlantic coast. The coolness of the climate, and briskness of the air, are confined to particular localities on the coast; and this description is not applicable to the interior of the country, or even to other places on the coast.

Such a hurry, such a bustle, so much excitement! We are nearing the wharf at San Francisco. What crowds of men assembled upon the pier, ready to rush on board as soon as the steamer is made fast! I almost envied those who were going to meet loved friends. We knew none, to give us a cheerful greeting, in that city of strangers.

Mrs. B——, a lady who was accompanied by her husband, and myself seated ourselves upon deck, to witness the meetings. So many joyful tears were shed, such heartful embraces! Fathers caressing little ones they had never before seen; they in turn frightened half out of their wits at finding themselves in the arms of such frightful objects. Sometimes we could scarcely repress the tears at witnessing some affecting scene; at others, constrained to laugh outright at some really ludicrous sight. One delighted husband said, "Why don't you kiss me, Bessy?" She stood gazing at this hirsute representation of her better half in utter astonishment; then timidly ejaculated, "I can't find any place." "Oh!" said Mrs. B——, sportively, "they will all get a kiss but you and me." Almost instantly a gentleman sprang to her side, cordially greeting her, and even bestowing a kiss. I was almost stupefied at such audacity, for at first she seemed not to recognize him. Soon the air of astonishment, and even of alarm, resigned its place upon her countenance to the glad smile of recognition. He was an old friend, whom she had not seen for years. He thought he recollected her countenance; then the sound of her voice confirmed his preconceptions. I felt greatly relieved when I found it was not the custom in California for the gentlemen to kiss all the ladies they fancied, whether acquainted or not.

My husband and myself, by invitation of the captain, concluded to remain on board that night. He insisted upon our occupying his room in his absence, as business called him ashore. "Everything," said he, "is at your disposal, except my tooth-brush."

Next morning, upon going ashore, my husband met a cousin of ours, who was residing in Happy

Valley. He came immediately on board, and insisted upon our going at once to his house. This cordial invitation we at once accepted. Mr. B—— had emigrated to California in 1849, and there married.

How unique to me seemed everything in San Francisco, when first I paced its sandy streets leading to Happy Valley! They were building up the water-lots rapidly. The old ship Niantic, of Boston, seemed quite up town. Upon the deck of this condemned ship was reared quite an imposing edifice, bearing the signature of the Niantic Hotel. Streets were extended far beyond it, bayward. The interstices between some of these streets were not yet filled. I grow dizzy even now, thinking about it. In our haste to reach Happy Valley, and avoid, as far as lay in our power, those interminable sand-hills, it was proposed to cross one of those interstices on a hewn timber, which, at least, must have been nearly one hundred feet, and at a height of twelve feet, I should think, from the green slimy mud of the dock. I succeeded pretty well, until about half-way over, when, finding myself suddenly becoming very dizzy, I was obliged to stop, get down on my knees, and hold on to the timber. I was afraid to proceed, lest I should fall into the mud and water below, and, for the same reason, unable to retrace my steps. After much crying on my part, and coaxing and scolding on the part of the gentleman, I succeeded in reaching the terminus of the timber. That was my introduction into the town of San Francisco in 1851.

Upon leaving, three years afterwards, I traversed that same locality. It had become the richest business part of the city. There were nicely paved walks, bounded on either side by massive granite and brick structures, an ornament to the city — the pride and the glory of the energetic pioneers, representatives from every state in the Union.

Very soon after our arrival occurred the largest conflagration ever recorded in the annals of San Francisco. The memorable fire of the 3d of May, 1851, will ever be remembered by all residents of the place at that time with feelings of pain and commiseration. Oh! it was a night of intense suffering to hundreds of human beings. We were startled from our slumbers between the hours of eleven and twelve, by the to me familiar cry of "Fire!" My first thought, upon awakening, was, "I am on terra firma, I can run." Fires, at that time of paper-and-cloth-architectural memory, raged with astonishing rapidity. Whole streets were swept away in less time than it would occupy to relate the events arising from the sad catastrophe. We were in Happy Valley, situated at that time at the extreme end of the town, towards Rincon Point. The fire originated as far in an opposite direction. Therefore people were all rushing towards Happy Valley, as a place offering protection.

The streets were full of drays, rushing along with breakneck speed, to deposit goods and all kinds of merchandise in any possible place of safety. What rich bales of silk, and fine clothing, were tumbled topsy-turvy into hastily made excavations in the innumerable sand-hills around the valley. Some were depositing valuables in the few (what were then supposed to be) fire-proof buildings, which had been erected at considerable expense. Often buildings were on fire before the inmates, in their consternation, could find an article of clothing; and they would rush into the crowded street in their night-clothes, nearly distracted with the deafening shouts of the excited multitude. The wind seemed to blow fiercely. The insatiable flames came roaring and rushing onward, darting its thousand-forked tongues of fire far up into the midnight sky. The fire companies, what few there were, were prompt and energetic in action; but even *they* were driven from their posts of duty, and their life-sacrificing efforts rendered abortive.

In one instance, a company, with their engine, were driven to the verge of a wharf by the fiery pursuer. Mrs. B—— and myself were standing upon the door-step, witnessing with trembling hearts its nearer approach and nearer. It was heart-rending to witness the distress of delicate women, driven from their homes at midnight, with no protection from the chilly winds but their night-clothes, lamenting, not their own fate, but the uncertain fate of those near and dear to them, who were combatting with the fiery elements for the preservation of life and property. Oh, it was a sad spectacle! Yet, even amid it all, might be seen some heartless person divesting himself of his own soiled apparel, to be replaced with new, purloined from some pile of ready-made clothing. How much of value, that night, the dishonest ones appropriated to their own use!

Still nearer came the flames, until only one block of buildings separated them from the Oriental Hotel. That once on fire, and no human power could save Happy Valley. All the engines were brought to play upon this block, which was owned by Macondry, and by him occupied as a warehouse. The bravely-fought struggle was viewed with varying emotions of hope and fear. At length the never-ceasing powers of man conquered. They succeeded in arresting the progress of the fire king, and the little hamlet of Happy Valley was preserved. At early dawn, we visited the scene of the fire. It would require a more graphic description than could ever emanate from pen of mine to do justice to the scene of destruction there presented. Lifeless bodies, literally burned to a cinder, wholly unrecognizable by nearest relatives, lay near to the walls of the half-demolished brick structure. They had fled to this building as a place of safety, thinking it to be, what all considered it, fire-proof. The flames raged around it with unresisting fury: the heat became very intense. The occupants vainly endeavored to effect an egress. One poor fellow rushed to remove the heated bolts, and actually burned all the flesh from his hands before effecting his object. Then he was seen to rush frantically forth into the flames, stagger, turn, and run a little way in an opposite direction — then fall. He was dragged from the flames by some daring, humane hand, and his life preserved; although he was maimed and crippled, and rendered blind, for life.

I saw the poor being afterwards, and heard him relate the painful story. The scenes I witnessed that day might wring tears from a heart of stone. Men who, a few short hours before, were worth thousands and hundreds of thousands, now sat weeping over the ashes of their once splendid fortunes. Some who were not possessed of sufficient self-command and fortitude to meet and brave life's severest trials, had sought consolation for every woe in the intoxicating cup; others sat, the images of mute despair, their grief too profound to permit a tear or sigh to escape as a mitigation of their deep-seated sorrow; some had already commenced fencing in their lots, although the smouldering ashes emitted an almost suffocating heat. These hasty proceedings were at that time expedient, to prevent their lots from being jumped; for these were the days of squatter memory, when possession was nine-tenths of the law. We were in pursuit of Mr. and Mrs. B——. With her I had formed a close intimacy on board the steamer. Her husband, previous to the fire, was established in a lucrative business, but who had now shared the fate of all. Where was Mrs. B—— and her little daughter Nelly? They were obliged to run in their night-clothes. Mr. B—— deposited two or three trunks of their most valuable clothing in one of those fire-proof buildings, and, of course, they were burnt, leaving them nothing which they could call their own out of their once abundant supply. Mrs. B—— that night sought and found protection at an hospital kept by a friend of hers, a doctor from New York. The building was situated upon the summit of one of the many hills which surround the city, and about a mile from where she had lived. This distance she ran, without even shoes or stockings, almost dragging her little girl along, who was so terrified as to be almost incapable of supporting herself. After learning her whereabouts, I hastened to see her, and found her, where she was obliged to remain for the time being, in bed. I supplied her with a few articles of clothing from my limited wardrobe; but she being a much taller person than myself, we were really at a loss how to make her appear respectable, unless she would consent to make her debut in Bloomer costume. "Necessity is indeed the mother of invention;" and, after some crying, and a good deal more laughing, we had her equipped for a promenade. Then Nelly was released from "durance vile;" but it would have puzzled wiser heads than ours to have designated her costume. Poor child! how she lamented the fate of all the nice things which she had brought from home! This was her first great grief. The proposition was made to us from Mr. and Mrs. B——, to go to housekeeping in company with them, and take boarders. No time was to be lost: after a fire in California was the time for immediate action. That day we found an unoccupied house, a little over the ridge of the hills.

The owner of this domicile had gone to the States; the agent for which was also absent in the mines. Therefore, our husbands had the audacity to take quiet possession; and, before night, we were duly installed in our new house. Perhaps some of my readers may have the curiosity to know how we so readily furnished our intended boarding-house, while nearly the entire city was in ruins. Well, in the house we found two bedsteads, with a miserable straw bed upon each; quite a good cooking-stove, with a few appurtenances attached; a pine table, constructed of unplaned boards; and old boxes, in lieu of chairs. Dishes, knives and forks, and spoons, we had picked up from the heterogeneous mass of half-consumed rubbish upon the former site of Mr. B——'s store. But, at such a time as that, if one could get anything to eat, he never stopped to see if his fork was blessed with one prong or three; and, if the knife was minus a handle, it was just as well, provided the blade was good. And then, too, a person was not particular about enjoying the luxury of both cup and saucer, if at any time there were more people than dishes. The next day, our husbands secured us as many boarders as we could accommodate with meals: a lodging they sought elsewhere.

We were to receive twelve dollars per week for board. Don't laugh: that was cheap board, when you take into consideration the exorbitant price of provisions. For butter we paid one dollar and a half per pound; beef steak, twenty-five cents per pound; and all else in proportion. Vegetables were sold by the pound, and dearly sold, too. I never prepared a meal, but what I thought of the old woman who had but one kettle in which to cook everything. We made coffee in the tea-kettle mornings; and, at night, made tea in the same.

There was a well of water at some distance from the house, near the foot of the hill; and, oh, what a deep one it was! The bucket, which would contain two pailfuls, had to be drawn to the top by a windlass. The united exertions of Mrs. B—— and myself were scarcely sufficient to bring it to the top. Oh, how we have laughed, and tugged, and laughed, until we could tug no longer, over that old well! Our husbands were busily engaged at the store-lot clearing and fencing it, and erecting a temporary building, to be in readiness to receive a fresh supply of goods which was daily expected to arrive, and which, fortunately for Mr. B——, had had a longer passage than usual. Our boarding-house in San Francisco will never be forgotten; and, when reverted to, will invariably call-up a smile, even if we are entertaining those provoking imps, the blues. Many times since, I have met some of those boarders at the tables of fashionable hotels; in which case, I was sure to receive some compliment in reference to the good dinners they had eaten from the old pine table, minus the table-cloth. The proceeds derived from keeping this boarding-house was decidedly insufficient remuneration for the amount of physical labor expended. We concluded, therefore, to seek our fortunes in some inland town, and nearer the mines, and perhaps at the mines.

CHAPTER XII.

About seven weeks from the time of our arrival in San Francisco, we found ourselves on board one of the river steamers bound to Marysville. I parted with regret from Mrs. B——. We had lived, and laughed, and suffered together *so* long, it was hard to separate. We met once afterwards, for she travelled many weary miles to visit me. Little Nelly, too — how I loved that child! I can see her now, in imagination, with her sparkling eyes and rosy cheeks, tugging along a handful of burnt wood for "mother to cook with." Those were hard days for Nelly and Mrs. B——. Since then, Mr. B—— has amassed a splendid fortune. I wonder if Nelly will ever forget those days in which she was sent out gleaning sticks of wood and pieces of burnt boards, with which to make the kettle boil.

The upper division of the bay of San Francisco is called the Suisun. Situated upon the strait connecting the two divisions, is the town of Benicia, on the north, and the pleasant little hamlet of Martinez, on the south side. How sunny and pleasant looked the valleys bordering on the bay! the luxuriant growth of wild oats therein affording excellent pasturage for the numerous herds of wild cattle roaming over the country. Soon we found ourselves entering the noble Sacramento. The river, at intervals, is fringed with timber, chiefly oak, sycamore, and willows. Grape-vines, and a variety of shrubbery, ornament its banks. The quiet, peaceful stillness which pervades all nature, as you are ascending this stream, has an ineffable charm, a sort of fascination, to the beholder. The boat stopped a short time at Sacramento city. How very low and flat the town appeared, in point of locality, compared with San Francisco, — not a single hill to relieve the eye! It presented one feature peculiar to all California towns at that day — a great deal of canvas pre-eminently conspicuous, in the shape of buildings, with signs attached, competing, in point of size, with the buildings which they graced.

In some places the river is nearly half a mile in width. It makes some very graceful bends. The land bordering on this magnificent stream is very low, and subject to inundations, which is a serious impediment to the advancement of agriculture, to which the soil is admirably adapted. Three years afterwards, when sailing down this majestic stream, I witnessed with delight many spots of this riverside wilderness, made to "blossom as the rose" by the indomitable energy and unconquerable enterprise, in opposition to every discouragement, of the successful pioneers. I often wished, as some spot lovelier than another met the eye, that it had been my lot to have found a home in just such a sunny spot, far away from the noisy strife of the busy, bustling world. But I must not tarry too long on thy bosom, noble Sacramento, but leave thy allurements and beauties to be chronicled by some abler pen than mine, and hasten up stream to the point where Feather River, one of the largest tributaries of the Sacramento, unites her limpid waters with those of her sister river.

With the name of Feather River the early Anglo-Californian associates the commingled sentiments of many a pleasure and pain. The rich tributes of gold which rewarded his toil could not compensate for the saddened yearnings of the heart. All that he loved on earth were far away from him; his condition was hazardous in the extreme; no friend, perhaps, was near with a solace; and, but for the inspiriting unction of a constantly indulged hope, even the *future* would have been desolate and dreary.

The steamer turns her prow to the right, and is

gracefully cutting her way through the waters of Feather River. I kept constantly upon deck to inhale the balmy air, and to look out upon the lovely and ever-changing landscape. Sometimes the trees would crowd the bank to the very brink; some gracefully bending to kiss the water; some rearing their stately heads high above, but stretching their wide arms over its margin; all faithfully mirrored far down in its glassy depth, though sometimes the reflections were partially obliterated, and sometimes, for a moment, the *whole* was shivered into trembling fragments by the transient breeze that swept the surface too roughly, and the widely extended ripple from the wake of the steamer.

There were on board several distinguished persons, who proposed a visit to Capt. Sutter's ranch. This delightful residence is situated on the left bank of Feather River, as you are proceeding up stream. Visitors of distinction are landed at the foot of his garden. The steamer runs in close proximity to the bank fronting his dwelling. They usually give him a salute after landing visitors. Sometimes an answering salute is given from a mounted cannon standing in the centre of his garden. Near to it is erected a tall flag-staff. The dwelling-house is constructed of adobe brick, representing the Dutch style of architecture. It is completely embowered with shrubbery, and creeping, flowering vines. A more definite description of the grounds adjoining will be given hereafter, when I shall have visited the place, and from personal observation endeavor to interest the reader by delineating the beauties surrounding this lovely retreat of the noble-hearted old general. Captain Sutter, or, rather, General Sutter, as he is now titled, is a native of Switzerland, and was at one time an officer in the French army.

He emigrated to the United States, and was naturalized. From thence, after a series of romantic incidents, he located himself in California, in the midst of numerous and hostile tribes of Indians. With a small party of men, which he originally brought with him, he succeeded in defending himself until he erected his fort. Several times, when besieged by hostile foes, he has subsisted upon grass alone for many days.

The land bordering upon Feather River is more elevated than that bordering upon the Sacramento. Soon, far ahead, is discernible the dividing line in the water, where the muddy waters of the Yuba River mingle with the deep, blue, translucent current of Feather River.

The banks of the Yuba, at its junction with Feather River, are romantic in the extreme. There is a thick growth of trees bestudding the banks, and dipping gracefully into the stream; the branches of the taller uniting overhead, and forming a leafy canopy, almost entirely excluding the rays of the sun from the smoothly gliding current. The beautiful weeping-willows fringing the margin, the creeping vines twining their tendrils around the trunks of the trees, and the variety of shrubbery, give it a decidedly tenebrious appearance, and keep the eye of the traveller, who gazes from the deck of some one of the numerous steamers plying the stream, constantly occupied in tracing the variety of features which this and similar views are constantly presenting.

A short distance above the cove-shaped entrance to the Yuba River, and at the head of steamboat navigation, is situated the town of Marysville. At the time I first saw it, the sun was just gilding the tops of the little canvas stores surrounding the plaza. This little square seemed literally swarming with people, who had gathered around the landing. Some had resorted thither from motives of idle curiosity, to gaze at the people as they stepped ashore, hoping, perhaps, to recognize the form and features of some friend from their far-off homes. Others were drawn to the spot in the hope of acquiring accessions to their already well-filled hotels. The draymen, too, were on the spot, ready to take your baggage anywhere and everywhere. Their importunities were as unceasing as those of our hackmen at city depots and steamboat wharfs. Their style of conveyance was rather more primitive than comfortable. However, I was seated upon my trunk on a dray, ready to be drawn to any one of the first-class houses, which were enumerated as follows: the United States, Oriental, Tremont, St. Charles, etc. My husband decided that we should go the United States, and thither we were accordingly taken.

I was perfectly delighted with the appearance of this little inland city. Every little collection of canvas stores and dwellings in California were denominated cities. Marysville, at that time, boasted of several large frame buildings, among which were the above-mentioned hotels. It was ranked the third city in regard to size and improvements in Upper California.

It is useless to attempt to convey to the minds of any, except those who were pioneers to California, the unique appearance of those little bustling, business localities, in convenient proximity to mining districts. Such trains of pack-mules as were constantly departing (so heavily laden, I pitied the poor beasts from my heart) on their long and tedious journeys to far-distant mining regions. There, too, is seen the swarthy Mexican vaquero, mounted on his fleet Californian steed, galloping through the street, " all booted and spurred ;"and oh, what spurs! — enough to make one cringe when they see them driven so mercilessly into the reeking sides of the poor beast. Then the mule and horse auctions at the corners of the streets, drawing together a motley-looking set of fellows, rough and uncouth in appearance, but possessing, nevertheless, noble hearts, ready hands, and, I have no doubt, well-filled purses, with which to assist a fellow-sufferer. I lived long enough in California to learn from experience never to judge a person by his apparel. The coarsest garb often covered the warmest hearts; the most sun-burned, heavily-bearded physiognomy often concealed the most intellectual features; for all classes had flocked indiscriminately to the gold regions of California.

On the night of our arrival, there was a travelling theatre to open for the first time in Marysville; and a mounted horseman was galloping through the streets, announcing, at the top of his voice, the programme of the evening's performance. After supper, being somewhat fatigued from the journey up river, I retired, but not to sleep. Such a din and confusion as was kept up in the street! A bowling alley and gambling house on the opposite side of the way each contributed their share to the babel-like confusion, that seemed to reign triumphant. Our room was situated in the front part of the building, the only access to which was from the balcony; and the only way of admitting any air into the room was by leaving open the door, which served the double purpose of window and door. Sometime in the night, we were aroused by some person moving about the room. I was terribly frightened, thinking, of course, it was some robber or assassin. My husband accosted the intruder with "Halloa! what do you want here?" The reply was, "I am coming to bed! what business have *you* in my bed? Come, vamos!" and, in the mean time, he was making preparations to strike a light. Said my husband, "There is a lady here; *we* occupy this room. Now leave instanter, or I will assist you." He started to the door, muttering, "I will see the landlord about this; if there was not a lady here, I would see who the room belonged to." As soon as he left, my husband shut and locked the door, and we were left unmolested, to smother until morning.

It seemed, upon inquiry, that our room had been previously occupied by two brothers. Upon our arrival, the house being crowded, and one of the brothers absent for a few days, the landlord had proposed to the remaining one to resign his double bed for a single one, in order to accommodate us. The absent brother returned late in the night, and the bar-keeper, through negligence or ignorance, omitted to inform him of the change; and thereby I was frightened half out of my wits at this midnight intrusion.

Ladies were very scarce in Marysville; at this time there were not more than half a dozen, at the most, who were deserving of the appellation. Comparatively speaking, there were no children. I had lived there more than a year before the merry voice of childhood gladdened my ears. There were no churches, no school-houses. All were intent upon the one great object that had lured them so far from their native land. There were assembled representatives from every clime and country on the face of the globe. The European, the Asiatic, the African, the Anglo-Saxon, the Sandwich-Islander, all, whose general interests and pursuits were so varied, had here convened for one and the same purpose — to get gold. No law was acknowledged except Lynch law; and the penalty for offences, so summarily enforced by the vigilance committees, served admirably to keep in check the murderous, villanous propensities of too many of the refugees from justice from all parts of the world. Alas! many of them had found a shelter in the almost inaccessible fastnesses of the mountains, remote from the regular settlements, and beyond the reach of organized vigilance committees. In the solitary recesses of the Sierra Nevada were little clusters of men, with nothing but the trees, and perhaps a little canvas tent, for shelter, and *no* protection but their own strength and vigilance, possessed of large amounts of gold, where there was no eye to see, and no agent to pursue, the guilty. It was not strange, where the temptation was so great, that robbers and assassins were ever ready to pounce upon the unwary.

Board at the United States Hotel at that time was four dollars per diem for the single person; therefore, with our limited means, we could remain here but a short time. The Tremont Hotel had been recently erected, and I learned the proprietors would like to find an American lady to superintend the domestic department. I presented myself, and obtained the situation. I was to receive one hundred and twenty-five dollars per month. In the interim, my husband was looking about, undetermined what business to engage in. We stopped at the Tremont five weeks, at the expiration of which time, my husband rented the Atlantic Hotel, and thither we removed. This was in July. The heat was intense, the thermometer ranging from 90 to 110 deg., not only day after day, but week after week. How I watched in vain for a cloud in the horizon! but not one appeared for months, to mitigate the scorching fervency of the heat.

While stopping at the Tremont, I witnessed what to me was a novel sight; and if, kind reader, you will pardon the digression, I will endeavor to relate, in a manner which I hope will interest, the method of taming a wild horse. The first I saw was an unusual collection of people, and in their midst a horse blindfolded, with a Mexican vaquero in the act of mounting. When once seated on the back of these wild, fleet animals of the plains, it is next to an impossibility to unhorse them. From the nature of their pursuits and amusements, they have brought horsemanship to a degree of perfection challenging admiration, and exciting astonishment. All things being in readiness, the blinder was removed. The horse, for the first time in his life feeling the weight of man upon his back, with distended nostrils, eyes glaring like orbs of fire, and appearing to protrude from their sockets, gave a succession of fierce snorts, performed sundry evolutions which would have puzzled the master of a gymnasium to have imitated, and then dashed off at a furious rate, seemingly determined to free himself from his captor, or die in the attempt. It was an exciting and cruel sport to witness. The reeking sides of the poor beast were covered with foam and blood, which had been drawn by driving those merciless spurs into the flesh. Both horse and rider would disappear for a few moments in some distant part of the town, then reappear again, dashing madly on. Finally, the horse, in passing the Tremont Hotel, which was all thrown open in front to admit air, sprang, quick as a flash, upon the piazza, and dashed madly into the bar-room. In making his ingress so suddenly, the Mexican's head had been forcibly struck against the top of the door, and he fell stunned to the floor. The inmates of the bar-room, numbering about twenty, fled in every direction. The bar-keeper, a very corpulent person, made his egress through a small back window — *so* small, that, upon ordinary occasions, he would never have had the presumption to attempt it, as it was actually endangering his life by so suddenly thrusting his portly figure through so small an aperture; but now, out of two evils, he was constrained to choose the least. The horse, finding himself in undisputed possession of the room, stood for an instant surveying himself in an extensive mirror suspended behind the long marble slab. Then, prompted by an irresistible desire to become better acquainted with the image reflected in the glass, or possessing the principles of teetotalism to such an extent that he was bent upon immediate annihilation, he dashed furiously at the bar, upsetting it, and dashing the splendid mirror into a thousand pieces, demolishing the elegant cut-glass decanters, while the contents ran profusely upon the floor. He also dashed to pieces several large arm-chairs, valued at twelve dollars apiece. Then he passed through a side-door into a large saloon, traversed that without doing any material damage; and, when in the act of leaving the house, the Mexican, who had, in the meantime, recovered his senses and his feet also, sprang with surprising agility upon his back, and the race for freedom again commenced; but this time not of long duration. The horse, reduced almost to prostration, yielded to the superior power of man, and was taken, more dead than alive, to a stable, rubbed down, placed in a stall, fed, and petted; and, from the hour in which he unwillingly relinquished a life of freedom, never more to roam with a wild herd over broad plains and flowery vales, he was a gentle, submissive slave. The wild horse is gracefully formed, with flowing tail and mane; but I never saw one very fat — they race their flesh off. The man who owned the horse readily paid the expenses of refitting the bar-room. The amount of property he destroyed was at that time estimated at a thousand dollars.

CHAPTER XIII.

The Sierra Nevada Mountains and the coast range run nearly parallel with the shores of the Pacific. The first are from one hundred to two hundred miles from the Pacific, and the last from fifty to sixty. The valley between them is the most fertile portion of California. Marysville is situated in this valley, about twenty miles in a south-westerly direction from the low hills of the Sierra Nevada; which form, as it were, the lower steps of an immense gigantic flight, terminating upon the summit of a range of mountains which would not suffer in comparison with any of transatlantic existence.

North of the city of Marysville is a plain of several miles in extent. This flat expanse is dotted with evergreen oaks, the shape and foliage of which, previous to minute examination, present an exact resemblance of the apple-tree. When it was impossible to procure apples at any price, or even after they were as low as fifty cents apiece, when enjoying a walk upon the plains I would be constrained, in opposition to my knowledge to the contrary, to look under the trees, wishing I could only find *one* apple, it would have tasted so sweet.

In a westerly direction from Marysville are situated the Butte Mountains, which present a singular appearance. They constitute one of the sublimest features of California scenery, rising as they do abruptly from the level plain which extends for miles around them. There are three high elevations, which, seen from a distance, might be aptly compared to three mountain islands, rising from the surface of the ocean. It is said that, standing on the top of the Butte Mountains in a clear day, with a telescope in hand, Monte Diabolo can be plainly seen: the space lying between is nearly three hundred miles. Feather River forms the western boundary to the city limits. The Yuba River opposite the plazza is wider than at any other place. When bank-full, I should judge it to be nearly three hundred yards in width. In the dry season, it is fordable for teams; and there is also a ferry across the river. The most of the city at first was built around the plazza, which is less elevated than the plain which extends back. Since then, owing to frequent inundations of the plazza, from which residents sustained material damage, they have removed most of the business houses to the upper part of the city. Marysville, I think, following the course of the river, is about two hundred miles, and perhaps two hundred and fifty, from San Francisco. The first rains there usually fall in November, and last until May. As soon as the ground becomes moistened, the grass, and other hardy vegetation, springs up; and, by the middle of December, the landscape is arrayed in a robe of fresh verdure; the plains, which, during the dry season, had assumed the appearance of the streets, now present a perfect carpet of green, as far as the eye can see. Beautiful flowers spring up spontaneously in every direction, gladdening the vision with their variegated and gorgeous colors, and, I wish I could add, rendering the air redolent with perfume; but, although so beautiful to the sight, they possess very little fragrance, if any.

Deep gullies that intersect the country, and which during the dry summer appear as if they never saw a drop of water, now become the channels of rapidly rushing streams. So much do they resemble rivers, that I heard one novice, who made his first appearance at this season, inquire, pointing to one of these sloughs, "Do they catch salmon in that river?" Some of them are deep and miry. Teamsters, who have attempted to ford them, have sometimes lost their lives in the attempt. When these sloughs are very much swollen by heavy rains, all communication with the country back is cut off. The season for sowing grain commences as soon as the ground is sufficiently moistened to permit of ploughing, and continues until March. There were some fine ranches along the banks of the Yuba. The bottom lands are very rich and productive, yielding an excellent harvest of wheat, oats, and barley. Vegetables grow to an enormous size, and surpass in flavor any I ever before tasted. I never dreamed of seeing water-melons grow to such a size as I saw them here. Recollect, now, I only state facts. I saw one water-melon sell for twelve dollars: it was sold by the pound. It was the first year any had ever been raised in Upper California. Mr. Briggs, who raised them, told me that that year, from the sale of his melons alone, he realized twenty thousand dollars. Is it to be wondered at that miners who had been subsisting one, two, and perhaps three years, upon pork and beans, and ham, varied occasionally by a repast of flap-jacks and molasses, and once in a great while get a sight of a potato, should be eager to possess themselves of a water-melon, at any price? No one except those who were miners in the early days of gold-hunting can conceive of the hardships, the sacrifices of the necessaries of life, and sometimes of life itself, they were subjected to — perhaps nearly starving, with thousands of dollars' worth of gold-dust in their possession. What will not a man suffer for gold? The first winter I passed in California proved to be the rainiest I ever afterwards experienced; yet that would scarcely compare with the winter of 1849.

I must confess I never before saw it rain (I should say pour) so unceasingly for such a length of time, — a week, perhaps, every day and night, and sometimes longer; then the sun would shine out quite warm for a week; then rain again. The mud in the streets was perfectly awful to behold, but much more awful to find yourself sinking into the miry depths. The rain in the valley was snow in the mountains; and, forty miles from Marysville, the snow might be ten feet deep or more, while in the city it would be sufficiently warm to sit with the windows open. When the dry season commences, then farewell to green grass, bright flowers, and everything pertaining to the beautiful, and prepare yourself to be suffocated with dust and sand, debilitated by the oppressive heat, and devoured by myriads of fleas. All this, and much more, you must endure, if you remain in Marysville through the summer. But, if not engaged in business, you can flee away to the mountains, and in some sequestered vale enjoy the lovely scenery, the cool spring water, inhale the invigorating mountain air, and, for exercise, climb to the summits of the mountains, timbered with large pines, firs, and cedars, with a smaller growth of magnolia, manzanita, hawthorn, etc., etc. Notwithstanding the heat is so intense during the dry season, the atmosphere is so pure that meat, when left exposed to the sun, never spoils; and, after one of those excessively hot days, the nights are extremely pleasant and comfortable. I never saw a night in California when I was deprived of refreshing slumber on account of the heat and oppressive atmosphere. I have known laboring men at work there digging cellars, when the thermometer in the place where they were at work would rise to 125 deg.; and yet those people could endure to work there, day after day, when, to work in such hot days in our climate, and with the sun striking directly on their heads, would have caused sickness, or even death.

It seemed so strange to me, after one of those hot days, not to see any appearance of a shower, not the slightest film of vapor in all the vast azure vault.

Some of the smaller houses were constructed of zinc. A lady who occupied one positively averred that the sides of the house were so hot, that she had only to place her dough, when she was going to bake bread, in close proximity to the wall, where the heat was sufficient to cook it. These zinc shanties were all abandoned before the summer was half spent. They were positively more like ovens than dwellings.

There is but little disease in the country arising from the climate. On some of the rivers, where vegetation is rank, and decays in autumn, the malaria produces chills and fever, which sometimes, when neglected too long, proves fatal.

The soil and climate of California is peculiarly adapted to the culture of the grape. The delicious richness and flavor of the California grapes nothing of the fruit kind can equal. The cactus grows spontaneously in California, and some of the inclosures are hedged in by this plant, which grows to an enormous size, and makes an impervious barrier against man and beast. The stalks of some of the plants are of the thickness of a man's body, and grow to the height of fifteen feet. One of the most serviceable of the California plants is the soap-plant. The root, which is the saponaceous portion of the plant, resembles the onion, and possesses the quality of cleansing linen equal to any soap.

The wild animals of California are the wild horse, elk, black-tailed deer, antelope, grisly bear, beaver, otter, cayote, hare squirrel, and a variety of other small animals. The interior lakes and rivers swarm with myriads of wild geese, ducks, and other birds; the pheasant and partridge are numerous in the mountains.

For salubrity I do not think there is any climate in the world superior to that of California. I have known people in the country who have been exposed much of the time to great hardships and privations, sleeping most of the time in the open air, and never suffering the first pangs of disease, or the slightest indications of ill-health. California is rich in mineral productions of all kinds.

Wheat, barley, and other grains, can be produced in the valleys without irrigation. Oats grow spontaneously, and with such rankness as to be considered a nuisance upon the soil. I have seen acres of these growing so high as to almost hide the cattle feeding among them. The oats grow to the summits of the hills, but not so tall as in the valleys. All the variety of grasses which cover the country are heavily seeded, and, when ripe, are as fattening to the stock as the grains with which we feed our stock in this country. Nearly all the fruits of temperate and tropical climates can be produced in perfection in California.

The Californians do not differ materially from the Mexicans, from whom they are descended. The native Californian is almost constantly on horseback, and, as horsemen, excel any I have seen in other parts of the world. The Californian saddle is the best that has ever been invented for the horse and rider. It is scarcely possible to be unseated by any ordinary casualty. The bridle-bit is clumsily made, but so constructed that the horse is compelled to obey the rider, upon the slightest intimation; the spurs are of immense size. With his horse and trappings, scrape and blankets, a piece of beef, and he is content, as far as personal comforts are concerned. His amusements consist of the fandango, game of monte, horse-racing, and bear and bull-fighting; and a very exciting sport among them is the lassoing of wild cattle. They are trained to the use of the lasso (riata, as it is here called) from their infancy. A vaquero, mounted on a trained horse, and provided with a lasso, proceeds to the place where the herd is grazing. Selecting an animal, he soon secures it by throwing the noose of the lasso over the horns, and fastening the other end around the pommel of the saddle. During the first struggles of the animal for liberty, which usually are very violent, the vaquero sits firmly in his seat, and keeps his horse in such a position that the fury and strength of the beast are wasted, without producing any other result than his own exhaustion. The animal, soon ascertaining that he cannot release himself from the rope, submits to be pulled along to the place of execution. Arriving here, the vaquero winds the lasso around the legs of the animal, and throws him to the ground, where he lies perfectly helpless and motionless. Dismounting from his horse, he then takes from his leggin his butcher-knife, which he always carries with him, and sticks him in the throat. The daring horsemanship, and the dexterous use of the lariat, usually displayed on these occasions, are worthy of admiration.

The native Californian ladies lack the clear, olive complexion so much admired in the pure Castilian; but they are equally as animated in conversation, and their dark eyes flash with all the intelligence and passion characteristic of the Spanish woman. There are few things more beautiful than their manner of salutation.

Among themselves, they never meet without embracing; but to men and strangers on the street they lift the right hand to near the lips, gently inclining the head toward it, and, gracefully fluttering their fingers, send forth their recognition with an arch beaming of the eye that is *almost* as bewitching as a kiss. They dance with much ease and grace: the waltz appears to be a favorite with them. Smoking is not prohibited in these assemblies, nor is it confined to the gentlemen. The cigarita is freely used by the señoras and señoritas; and they puff it with much gusto while threading the mazes of the cotillon, or swinging in the bewitching waltz. The cigarita is not without its powers of fascination in the lips of a lovely woman, even rivalling the use of the fan as an appliance of coquetry.

In Marysville were assembled women from all parts of the world; and I assure you it was an interesting study to watch the different natures, dispositions, tastes, pursuits, manners, and customs of these fair representatives of distant climes. But among them all, the Yankee women stand preeminent, so far as regards principle, industry, and economy, and, as a general thing, are as often sought after for companions for life by the opposite sex as those who can claim preëminence in mere personal attractions, and are destitute of the more sterling attributes, so essential to prosperity and happiness through the varied phases of real life.

CHAPTER XVII.

I WILL now give you a sketch of our hotel-keeping in California. My husband rented the Atlantic Hotel, which was not a very spacious one, for two hundred and twenty-five dollars per month. For our cook we paid two hundred and fifty per month, our steward one hundred and twenty-five, and for all other assistance in a similar proportion.

The house was always filled to its utmost capacity; and the prospect of future success was flattering in the extreme, provided I had strength given me to sustain the weight of care and labor necessarily devolving upon me. Often, on account of exorbitant demands from servants, — demands which could not reasonably be granted, — I would be compelled to work early and late, for days and weeks in succession. Not having been accustomed to living and working in such excessive heat, my system became debilitated; I felt my strength gradually yielding to excessive weakness; and, in a little less than three months from the time we went to the Atlantic, I was seized with a fever. For weeks I lay very sick. My physician pronounced my recovery hopeless unless removed from the hotel, where, of necessity, so much confusion prevailed. Consequently, I was removed to a little canvas shanty, which my husband had previously purchased, placed upon a straw bed, and for more than two months I was confined to that pallet of straw.

The dimensions of the lot upon which this shanty was erected were one hundred and sixty by eighty feet. It was represented to be an excellent location, destined to be soon in the heart of a big city. My husband paid four hundred dollars for the place; and, as an evidence of the sudden and enormous rise of real estate in California, where there was the least prospect of a city rushing into existence, — for in that country cities have no state of infancy, — I will here add, that, three years afterwards, this same lot, with the addition of a better building, though not an expensive one, was valued at twelve thousand dollars, and could have been disposed of quickly for that sum. During the two months that I was prostrated by sickness, my sufferings were intense, both physical and mental. Doctors at that time were charging five and eight dollars a visit. The state of the country was such, it was almost impossible to procure the comforts of life, unless one was possessed of a fortune.

Eggs were seven dollars per dozen; milk, one dollar per quart; and, for six weeks, I was not allowed to eat any thing except boiled milk. Our income had ceased when we sold out the hotel. Every day my disorder was growing worse, and our funds were growing less. The sides of our little shanty were constructed of rough clapboards, not very nicely matched; in some places, you could put your hand through the interstices. The roof was canvas, and miserably old at that. The front part of this domicile could boast of a few boards, which served as an apology for a floor. Old boxes and trunks served in lieu of chairs. When I was able to sit up, there was no chair to sit in. My husband procured one at Sacramento, — quite an inferior cane-seated rocking-chair, — for which he paid the exorbitant sum of twelve dollars. That was the first and only chair which ever graced our miserable abode. My bed and even pillows were of straw; and oh, how hard they seemed to my poor and emaciated frame! for I was reduced to a mere skeleton. At times, when the fever raged, how grateful I should have been for one drop of cold water. All the water with which the city was supplied was taken from the Yuba River. It was quite warm, and rendered far from clear by the mining operations which were carried on at the bars above. The painful sickness which chained me for so many weeks to a sick bed was superinduced by drinking too freely of this muddy water.

In close proximity to our dwelling was a second-class boarding-house, from which, especially at night, issued discordant sounds of noisy revelry, mingled with angry bickerings. All this was peculiarly trying to one whose nerves were wrought to the utmost tension. When nights I would be left alone for hours together, I suffered inconceivably from fright. When my husband would go out, he would lock the door upon the outside; for I was too feeble to rise from the bed without assistance, and far too timid to remain alone with the doors unfastened. Every fresh burst of uproarious mirth or frightful anger issuing from the contiguous building would send a thrill of horror through my veins. Oh, how my thoughts, during those lonely nights, would wander to my home! How my heart yearned for the soothing words and kind attentions, so soul-cheering when emanating from the sympathetic bosoms of disinterested and tender friends! All this was denied me. I had formed no female acquaintances in this place. There was no one to come and smooth my hard pillow, or utter cheering, consoling words. The present was dark and dreary, with no bright star beaming through the murky horizon of the future. One day I was no less pleased than surprised at the appearance of a lady in my room, whose benevolent, pleasant countenance plainly implied peace, hope, and happiness. She introduced herself as Mrs. S——, recently from Cincinnati. Her residence being near, she had accidentally heard of my situation, and had visited me for the express purpose of rendering any assistance in her power. No kind mother could have been more attentive to the wants of a loved child, than was Mrs. S—— to mine through the remainder of my sickness. She had her own family to attend to; yet every day she found time to visit me, and minister kindly to my wants. How anxiously I watched for her coming! and when I would hear her light footstep, and listen to the gentle accents of her sweet voice, I could only acknowledge her presence but by tears. She was a messenger of peace and love, a truly pious and exemplary woman, and, during my residence in Marysville, ever remained my firmest friend. She prospered in Marysville; and may kind Providence *ever* shower His richest blessings upon this truly Christian lady!

About this time the country was unusually agitated. The villanies practised and murders committed by an organized band of cut-throats, of whom the notorious mountain robber, Joaquin, was the chief, had excited the horror, and aroused the vengeance, of the entire populace of Upper California. No effort had been spared to capture him, dead or alive; but, with the perfect adroitness of an accomplished scamp, he ever eluded and bid defiance to pursuit by mounting some one of the many fleet steeds at his command, and fleeing to the almost inaccessible fastnesses of the mountains. His path was ever stained with human blood. A reward of one thousand dollars for the apprehension of Joaquin, offered by Governor Bigler, was still further increased by the sum of three thousand added to it by the Chinese. These people are industrious, economical, and timid. It was ever the policy of Joaquin and his associates to prey with particular severity upon the Chinese. Frequent thefts were committed in their camps; and, when resistance was attempted, they were butchered with a heartless cruelty, becoming the sanguinary nature of the murderer and outlaw. When suddenly surprised, he would boldly face his enemies, and receive their bullets on his breast, which glanced or were flattened by a coat of steel worn underneath his clothing.

All Spanish countries have their guerillas and ladrones; but a feature of this kind, precipitated into American communities, and attended with such unparalleled atrocities, without the power of the people to avenge, was something astonishingly rare indeed. California was not the place of his birth, and he could not, therefore, have had any national jealousies because of the occupancy of the country by the Americans. He seemed to murder merely for the love of the sport, and to rob because it was a life of excitement, requiring great risk in its accomplishment, and yielding large profits when attended with good luck. But his career of villany was limited; and, when he least expected it, he was seized upon to expiate his crimes by an ignominious death. But I am anticipating. One night, I was excessively alarmed by an unusual commotion about the town. Ringing of bells, galloping of horses, groups of people rushing past, talking fiercely,— all conspired to confirm the belief in my mind, that the vigilance committee were about to execute summary punishment upon some guilty offender. I awoke my husband: he dressed himself as quickly as possible, and issued forth to ascertain the occasion of so much noise. Locking the door after him, he walked away to join the throng of people collected around a large hardware store at the corner of the street. He was gone so long, I feared some accident had befallen him. What agonizing doubts I was a prey to while lying in suspense in that little shanty! It was a long time before he returned. He finally came with the intelligence that Joaquin, with several of his accomplices, were encamped about three miles out from Marysville, at a place called the Sonorian Camp; and that Sheriff Buchanan, in attempting to surprise and capture him, had been shot.

A few days previous to this, the citizens of Marysville and vicinity had been horribly shocked by the announcement in their midst of a cruel murder, perpetrated on the road between Hansonville and Marysville. A citizen of Marysville had carried a load of goods to Hansonville, and disposed of them for the sum of fifteen hundred dollars. On his return, he was pursued and overtaken by some Mexicans, supposed to be of Joaquin's band, lariated and drawn from his wagon, and mangled in a horrible manner. On the same day, a passenger wagon was intercepted, and every passenger murdered; even the horses' throats were cut. And now this last deed had aroused the spirit of revenge in the breast of every one capable of carrying arms.

The particulars of the affair were these: That night, a little Mexican boy, who resided at the Sonorian Camp, prompted by feelings of revenge for a punishment that day received, came to the sheriff, and revealed Joaquin's place of concealment. Buchanan, eager, doubtless, of achieving unparalleled renown by capturing this notorious robber chieftain, with a select few hastened to the spot designated by the boy. In their march, they were compelled to step over a fallen tree lying immediately in their path. - They had no sooner planted their feet upon the trunk of the tree, when a dozen armed men sprang to confront them, and discharged their revolvers in their faces. The consternation of the sheriff and his party was universal. Those of the number who were not so disabled as to prevent escape, beat a hasty retreat. Among these was Buchanan. He had not fled many paces, when he received a mortal wound, as he supposed, which brought him to the ground. He was dragged along by his companions to the Sonorian Camp, where a litter was procured, upon which he was transported to his home in town. Three or four hundred of the inhabitants armed themselves with fire-arms from the hardware store above alluded to, and proceeded to the ambuscade of the terrible robber chief. My husband departed with the troop, previously locking me into the little shanty; for I dared not remain for an instant, in such exciting times, with the door unfastened. For fear he would not return in the morning before the heat became too oppressive for me to bear, he raised a window in the room, and dropped the curtain. Then I was alone, a prey to my gloomy fancies. Every noise I heard, I fancied was from some terrible Mexican effecting an entrance through the window, and, in imagination, could already discern the swarthy, murderous visage, and detect the sharp, glittering blade of the assassin's knife. The memory of that night, even now, is accompanied with a shudder. Soon daylight began to dawn, and with the shades of night vanished all my fears. I was so weakened by sickness, that, like a child, who is naturally prone to superstition and fear when alone in the dark, the sufferings I endured that night were similar. The forenoon crept on apace, and yet that band of armed men had not returned, I knew, by the silence which reigned in the streets. As I lay, wishing my husband would return, the window-curtain parted suddenly, and one of the ugliest-looking faces was thrust into the room I ever beheld. At first, I was nearly paralyzed with terror; then, recovering my faculties, I exclaimed, at the top of my voice, "Vamos! vamos!" Knowing him to be Spanish by his look, I addressed him in his own language; yet, feeling that was not sufficiently expressive, I added, by way of effect, a few English invectives, which fell *very* harmlessly upon his uncomprehending ear. I have often since been amused at the recollection of the amount of courage displayed in words, when I was so entirely helpless and imbecile, as far as action was required. He very leisurely reconnoitred the apartment, cast a look commingled of scorn and pity upon me, turned upon his heel, and disappeared. What was the object of this visit of espionage, I never could conjecture. About noon, my husband returned. The party had been unsuccessful in the pursuit; had caught glimpses of the retreating party several times, but they had finally eluded pursuit. The people returned chagrined and discomfited to their homes, to hear, in a week, of other murders still more atrocious. The sheriff was alive at noon, but no hopes were entertained of his recovery, as the ball, to all appearance, had entered his side, and passed out at the breast. His friends stood around the bed, momentarily expecting him to breathe his last; still he lived on. His physician concluded to probe the wound, and found that the ball, upon entering, had struck a rib, glanced and followed the rib around, and passed out in front. In a few days he recovered his health, resumed his official duties, and continued them long after that.

Oh, how happy I felt when I could walk out once more! Distinctly do I recollect the first day I left the shanty for a walk. I went the distance of a square to visit my kind friend Mrs. S——. Upon my return, I found a dear brother whom I had not seen for two years and more. Oh, the joy of that meeting! Words would inadequately express my feelings. Only one month had elapsed since he bade adieu to home and friends, laden with so many messages of love; and now here he was, beside me, repeating what father, mother, brothers, sister, had said such a short time ago. It seemed as if I had been transported to the dear old home; had met the family assembled around the hearthstone, and together we had spoken sweet words of counsel and of love. The night succeeding his arrival, we sat and conversed together until daylight began to dawn, we had so much to say — *I* so many questions to ask; *he* so much to relate. He was very much shocked to see me looking so much like a wreck of my former self. Sickness and trouble — yes, *such* trouble as rankles deepest in the heart of a wife, compared with which, death would have been joy — was fast doing its work.

CHAPTER XV.

Soon after my brother's arrival, I received a visit from my esteemed friends, Mr. and Mrs. B—— and Nelly. During their stay, we visited Yuba city, situated about half a mile from Marysville, on the opposite bank of Feather River. It may not be amiss to state, that Yuba city, with the exception of three or four houses, has been removed to Marysville. There is, however, an Indian rancheria existing there, which draws many visitors to the spot. We started, one bright morning, in a two-horse team, to visit the rancheria. It was proposed to ford the stream. Accordingly, we started for the ford. The banks of the river are quite precipitous; and, as we descended the steep slope, and saw the wide, rolling river below, we felt (Mrs. B—— and myself) as though we would rather never see an

Indian rancheria than stem the swiftly rushing current; but soon down we went with such a rush, we could not tell where we were until the water around our feet caused us to suspect we were really sinking. The river proved to be higher than our driver anticipated, or the wagon not as high, and by the means we reached the opposite bank a wetter, if not a wiser party.

An Indian rancheria consists of a number of huts, constructed of a rib-work or frame of small poles, or saplings of a conical shape, covered with grass, straw, or tule, a species of rush, which grows to the height of five or six feet. The huts are sometimes fifteen feet in diameter at their bases, and the number of them grouped together vary according to the number of the tribe which inhabit them. The Indians are generally well made, and of good stature, varying from five feet four inches to five feet ten, with strong muscular developments. Their hair is long, black, and coarse; and their skin is a shade lighter than that of a mulatto. It is universally conceded that the California Indians possess but few, if any, of those nobly daring traits of character which have distinguished the savage tribes of the Atlantic States, from the days of King Philip down to the notorious Billy Bowlegs.

The extreme indolence of their nature, the squalid condition in which they live, the pusilanimity of their sports, and the general imbecility of their intellects, render them rather objects of contempt than admiration. They are deficient in all those manly arts which have given measurable immortality to the Cherokees. They have none of the invention of the Sioux, Pottawatamies, or other north-western Indians, and are outwitted by the cunning even of the "Tontos," whose own self-applied vernacular assigns no higher rank in aboriginal tradition than that of *fools*.

They place entire dependence on nature's bounty for support. If the crop of acorns fails, or the mountain streams send not forth their usual schools of fish, — snails, worms, roots, and insects, furnish food with which they appease the gnawings of hunger. There is a kind of grass in the valleys the Indians eat, that is pleasant to the taste and nutritious. In the season of this grass, I have seen numbers of them all out feeding like cattle. The children all go naked. This grass has a tendency to increase their ordinary dimensions; and you will often hear it remarked, as one makes his appearance, "There comes a little grass-fed." We saw them making their acorn bread (parn they call bread). To render it short and rich, they mashed up angle-worms, and put in it. After baking it,— which they did by making an excavation in the earth, and building a fire therein; when the earth was sufficiently heated, they scraped out the ashes, put in the bread, and covered it over with hot ashes,— they generously insisted upon our eating a piece. The keenness of our appetites was considerably repressed, however, by witnessing the several employments of the tribe. One old squaw was relieving her husband's head of a score of vermin, which she ate with an apparent relish. She practised, however, the principle of self-abnegation to perfection, by occasionally tossing some of the finest-looking ones down his throat, for which he smacked his thanks with apparent zest. The hair on the heads of the chiefs is all drawn up, and tied in a knot on the top of the head, and ornamented with feathers. The squaws' heads look like pitch-mops; the hair is very thick, coarse, and black, and cut square round the head. No part of the forehead is visible; the hair falls to the eye-brows. They have jet-black eyes; and some of them have a decidedly pleasant expression with the eye. The little babies are beauties. Their mothers learn them to swim, as soon as an old duck does her young. They build little pens at the brink of the river, so that the current cannot carry them down stream, put them in, and keep them there half the time. They are really amphibious. They have a cruel custom of piercing the ears of their infants, and inserting sticks the size of the little finger. During the process of thus beautifying their infants, the whole side of the head and face is terribly swollen, and the child must suffer inconceivably; but better for them to die in the operation than to live in opposition to the prevailing mode.

The longevity of the race is proverbial. We saw some who looked more like mummies than living beings. They bring them out of the huts, and set them in the sun, days; and there we saw them sitting, their eyelids drooping so you could not perceive the eyeball, limbs perfectly motionless, and so shrivelled and black as to be absolutely repulsive to the sight. Some of their limbs are affected with a loathsome cutaneous disease.

When one of their number dies, they consume the body by fire, grind the bones to ashes; then the near relations mix these ashes with pitch, and daub their heads and faces with it, as a badge of mourning. During this process, and for several consecutive days and nights, they keep up a loud hooting and howling, and render night hideous with their mournful lamentations. They have large gatherings sometimes at their rancherias, to celebrate some event; then dancing and singing, loud shouting and howling, is continued without intermission the whole night. During these orgies, the noise made by them is such as to prevent sleep, although a quarter of a mile distant. Their council-chamber is of sufficient capacity to accommodate three hundred persons; the entrance to which is an aperture of just sufficient size to admit a man's body when bent double. In the centre of the roof is another small aperture; and, except by these two openings, no air or light can be admitted. They perform their singular dances in this place. Often Americans go there to witness these sports; but a few moments' confinement in such a close place generally suffices. From their burrowing propensities, these Indians have derived the name of "Diggers."

Their mode of costume almost defies description, it is so omnifarious. Sometimes they imitate the style adopted by our first parents in Paradise. The women are especially delighted to get on a man's shirt, in which they will parade the streets apparently as pleased with themselves as any fashionable belle when sporting the most costly fabric. I was once exceedingly amused at the sight of an Indian and his squaw promenading the street, dressed à la mode. He sported a pair of boots, and an old, faded piece of calico over his shoulders, as an apology for a serape. She was dressed in a red flannel shirt, over which she had drawn an old black satin sack, which some one had given her, or which she had stolen. Over their black heads was elevated a shattered umbrella, and her arm was placed within his. Immediately in advance of them were walking a very fashionably dressed gentleman and lady. The countenances of the "Digger" and his mehala (an appellation given to the squaws) were illuminated with a grin expressive of much delight, entertaining, no doubt, the satisfactory belief that they were equally as much admired by observers as those in advance of them, whose motions and walk they were vainly endeavoring to imitate. They are inveterate gamblers; but I think it would puzzle wiser heads than mine to understand their games. They appear to place some value upon money, with which they gratify their gambling propensities. They flock in numbers into the back yards of hotels, and greedily devour all the offal destined to be thrown to the hogs. Sometimes you can induce them to cut a few sticks of wood; but, as a general thing, they are too indolent to exert themselves much.

The rivers abound in excellent salmon, which the Indians spear in great numbers, and dispose of in the towns. They are the finest I ever tasted. Some of them are three and four feet long, and weigh fifty pounds or more. It is amusing to see the Indians spearing them. They stand in the river on rocks or shoal places, looking intently into the water with the spear elevated, waiting, perfectly motionless, for a sight at one. Instantly the spear descends, and, as sure as it does, it buries itself in the body of the fish. Their aim is unerring.

CHAPTER XVI.

At this time my husband was engaged in transporting goods to the towns above Marysville. He kept his horses in a shed at the rear of our dwelling. One night we were aroused by the cry of "Fire!" Upon opening my eyes, the room was as light as day. It appeared as if the whole city was in a blaze. The flames were rapidly spreading. Those light wood and canvas buildings offered but slight resistance to the fiery element. Our first thought was of the horses and wagon, as they were of more value than the house, or all it contained. They were given into my charge, with instructions to lead them away out on the plains, and hold them there, while they remained to throw what few things we possessed into the wagon, and drag it off. The most valuable article in the house was my side-saddle, for which was paid the sum of sixty-five dollars. That, in their haste, was forgotten, and left in the house. I had petted those horses so much, they would follow me anywhere. They stood perfectly quiet beside me, apparently watching with me the progress of the fire. I expected, of course, our little shanty had shared the fate of half the buildings of the place. After the fire had subsided, we returned to town; and there, sure enough, stood the little house unharmed, while all on the opposite side of the street lay a heap of ruins. In one week from that time, very nearly the same scene was enacted over again.

This time, too, the canvas shanty welcomed us back again to town. Had it been of any value, perhaps it would have shared the fate of its neighbors; but, valueless as it was, it looked better to me upon my return than a mass of smoking ruins in lieu. What oversights a person will commit when alarmed, or agitated by the cry of "Fire!" One of these nights I dressed myself hastily, put on my dress (which fastened in front) hind-side before, and fastened every hook securely. Of course, I never discovered my mistake until I returned to the house. Soon after this, my brother left for the mines. When the 'rainy season commenced, our house was a poor protection from the rain. It ran through the canvas roof as through an old sieve. We soon vacated it, and went to the Oriental Hotel. This building my husband rented for the sum of six hundred dollars per month, furniture included. It was a spacious new building, at that time the finest in the place. Our expenses were eighteen hundred dollars per month. We employed three cooks. To our head cook we gave three hundred per month, and all the other domestics in a like proportion. To one little boy, not much higher than the table, who was employed to wait upon the cooks, clean knives and forks, bring in wood, etc., we paid the exorbitant sum of sixty-five dollars per month. Notwithstanding our expenses were so much, the net profits were ample.

We had twenty and twenty-five dollars per week for board. The house was always crowded. While we were at the Oriental Hotel, the city was inundated. Oh, that was indeed a gloomy time! A vast amount of property was destroyed, and some lives lost. The sudden melting of the snow in the mountains swelled the mountain streams to rushing torrents. The most intense excitement prevailed in Marysville, as the Yuba River, swollen to its utmost capacity, was still rapidly rising. What a wildly rushing, roaring, foaming mass of water came thundering on! Higher and yet higher it came, until the plaza was fairly submerged. Trucks were rushing to and fro, laden with merchandise being conveyed to the upper part of the city. Many objected to leaving their houses, thinking the water would abate, until they were obliged to make their egress through the windows, and in boats were taken to dry land. The Oriental fronted on quite high land. At the back was a large basement, where was situated the culinary department, also the servants' apartments. All this part of the building was entirely submerged, and the water lacked but a few inches of being to the first floor. Night was coming on, and the water was still rising. Fear and anxiety sat enthroned upon the countenances of all. A short time previous to this, there had been erected on the plaza two brick blocks. The water undermined the foundation of these buildings, and that night they fell with a terrible crash. It is almost impossible to convey to the minds of those not present any correct idea of the gloomy aspect of affairs during the inundation. Towards morning, the waters ceased to rise any higher, yet did not subside in the least. A man residing on a ranch about five miles above Marysville, in attempting to save some cattle from drowning, was swept from his horse by the force of the current, and was borne down stream with astonishing rapidity. He managed to keep his head above water, but was unable to clutch at anything whereby he might save himself. As he neared the landing at Marysville, all the latent energy of his being was aroused to save his life, as that would be his last chance. There was a large steamer lying there, made fast to the big tree on the plaza. Any one who has visited Marysville will recollect this venerable tree. Some of the earliest pioneers to this place recognize it as an old friend, under whose protecting arms they have for many nights sought a shelter. With almost superhuman exertions, he caught hold of one of the paddle-wheels of the steamer, and maintained his position until rescued by some people who had seen him struggling in the water.

Feather River, too, overflowed her banks, and, in a south and westerly direction from Marysville, nothing could be seen but one unbroken sheet of water. Many of the smaller houses were washed down stream. One couple, living on a ranch twenty miles from Marysville, on the bank of Feather River, and far from any other habitation, were driven for safety to the top of a table. As the water rose higher, they were obliged to rise higher. It was a little bit of a shanty. They knocked a hole through the roof, and crept out thereon. They soon found they must vamos from there; so they embarked in some sort of a craft (tub or barrel), and paddled off to a little island. After congratulating themselves upon their miraculous escape, they found they were not the only occupants of this island retreat: a big grisly bear had preceded them. Not relishing such close companionship as he seemed inclined to offer, they quickly beat a retreat to a large tree, and, seated in its topmost branches, carefully guarded by "Old Bruin," they passed twenty-four gloomy hours. When assistance arrived from a neighboring ranch, in the shape of a boat well manned, it was Bruin's turn to beat a retreat, which he did. The frightened, hungry couple were released from their perilous situation.

My brother had returned from the mines, and was living upon a ranch on the banks of the Yuba. He swam his horse quite a distance to save a woman and child. When he arrived at the shanty, they were perched upon a table, calmly awaiting their fate.

The boats were sailing in every direction about the city; and all through the night could be heard the shrill cry of "Boat, ahoy!" resounding far over the waters. All night long, on the opposite side of the Yuba, sat a Spaniard on the ridge-pole of his house, at one end, while, at the other end, was a big rat, each anxiously expecting relief.

Very gradually the waters began to subside; but it was a week before the city was passable at all. One small house which was washed down stream, and lodged some distance below, the owner afterwards recovered; and, after placing it upon its original site, he corralled it, for fear of a similar accident.

We kept the Oriental four or five months; but the numerous cares devolving upon me were too wearing for my constitution. Could I have been relieved from so much anxious solicitude, we should have remained in the house longer. Now the rainy season was nearly over, we returned to our little shanty.

CHAPTER XVII.

ABOUT this time, in company with my brother, I took a journey a distance of eighty miles up the Sacramento River. The whole distance, the route lay through the most beautiful valley of which imagination can conceive. It was the season for flowers, and in every direction the most beautiful floral blossoms met the eye. Oh, the beautiful ranches (farms we should call them) that were situated on the banks of this magnificent stream! We passed some fields of wheat, containing five hundred acres in one inclosure. We forded numerous streams which intercepted our course. We saw herds of antelope bounding gracefully from our path. To some we got sufficiently near to see their clear, bright, shining eyes. Their graceful symmetry of form, their agile, sylph-like motions, all combine to render them one of the most beautiful animals in the country. The fawn of the American deer, if captured before the pretty white spots upon its sides have disappeared, will follow its captor anywhere, if he will first carry it a little while in his arms. They are the perfection of grace, innocence, and confidence. Probably there is no wild animal more susceptible of domestication, when taken young, than the American deer.

We saw, too, the elk, in large numbers. Once, as we were approaching a stream, there were several drinking therefrom. As soon as they perceived us, they reared aloft their heads, surmounted by huge and stately antlers, and dashed away with the velocity of the wind. As we neared a ranch belonging to Mr. N——, everything bespoke the wealth and prosperity of the ranchholder. He possessed a herd of one thousand horses. That day they were corralled, for the purpose of branding those not already bearing the owner's mark. This seems to me a cruel process, yet an unavoidable one there, where so many different people's stock are running together over the plains. They blindfold the beast, and chain it to a post deeply imbedded in the earth. Then the blacksmith takes the branding-iron, bearing the owner's stamp, heats it red hot, and applies it quickly to the shoulder or haunch of the animal. How the seared hair and hide smoke! and how the poor creature plunges and rears with fright and pain! I have too much sympathy for the poor brutes ever to be a ranch-holder, or the wife of one. We dined at the ranch of Mr. L——, whose waving fields of grain, with other appurtenances, revealed in a measure the extent of his wealth.

We travelled on through elysian valleys, until we reached our destination. The only objection a person could have to a residence in these sunny vales is the annoyance one is subjected to from myriads of musquetoes, which, at certain seasons, swarm the country. I have seen laborers at work in the fields with green veils tied to their hats, and drawn down over their faces, and fastened about their necks. When we reached our destination (the ranch of Mr. S——), I was very much fatigued; but that, in a measure, was dispelled by the hearty welcome I received from Mrs. B—— (Mr. S——'s daughter), an interesting lady from New York, who arrived in the country at the time I did. Her father was a very wealthy ranchholder.

Their dwelling-house was constructed of adobe brick. It was only one story high, but more than sixty feet long. Mr. S—— employed a host of Indians upon his ranch. The beautiful gardens and extensive fields of grain furnished convincing proofs of the enterprise, industry, and energy of the proprietor. Nineteen years' salutary training had, in a measure, eradicated the indolent propensities inherent to the Digger race. Mr. S—— had been a resident in California, and on that ranch, for nineteen long years. What caused him to leave his family and native land, to seek a home in the wilds of California, is unknown to me. But so he did. When he left his home, Mrs. B——, the daughter then with him, was a babe scarcely six months old. During those long years of separation, the wife knew not the whereabouts of her husband, or of his existence even. His little children grew to man's and woman's estate in the interim, never dreaming they had a father in California. Some were old enough to recollect him before his self-banishment from their presence; but they soon learned to speak of him as one gone to the spirit-land.

One chill autumn eve in 1850, might have been seen a man a little past the meridian of life, whose silvered locks and furrowed cheeks gave evidence of past griefs, of sufferings that had roughly stirred the deep fountains within, — else the surface would not have been so deeply channelled, — standing irresolutely before the door of a neat mansion in New York city. Conflicting emotions of pleasure and of pain were rapidly crossing each other upon his countenance; and well they might, for he was standing, after an absence of nineteen years, at the door of his own house, desiring, yet scarcely daring, to enter. He summoned courage to ring; the door opened, and he crossed the threshold of his home, — confronted his wife — how changed from the young and blooming woman he left so long ago! yet, the instant their eyes met, the recognition was mutual. The little Bessy he left a babe, was all the child remaining at home. He remained with his wife and child that winter; but there existed a yearning for his home in California, that he vainly endeavored to conquer. He must return. Would his wife and child go with him? The daughter would, for she manifested unusual affection for her father, so recently found. The wife preferred to remain behind. In the spring, father and daughter left New York for the home in California. They were unavoidably detained at Panama. While there, the daughter became acquainted with a young gentleman from her native city. He proposed, was accepted, and they were united at Panama, before proceeding on their voyage. And here they were domesticated, away in the interior of California. They appeared to be enjoying as much happiness as ever falls to the lot of mortals. How pleasant it seemed to enter that adobe building, and find everything arranged with a neatness and regularity eliciting admiration. Mrs. B—— performed no household duties herself. She had five or six well-trained Indian women for house servants, who labored hard for no other remuneration than their food and raiment. The last-mentioned stipulation, however, was easily complied with, as they require but very little clothing — just as much as decency requires, and no more.

Mrs. B—— is a lovely woman, well qualified to grace the most refined and intelligent society. There was a novelty and charm connected with their residence in that remote place, which rendered life peculiarly pleasant. The extensive tract of land which Mr. S. possessed (since the confirmation of the ranch titles) has rendered him immensely wealthy. Immediately upon our arrival, our horses were allowed to revel in the luxuries of wild oats. They were actually up to their eyes in acres of the nutritious grain. After the business which had led us to that remote place had been ratified, we started on our homeward journey, with much more extended views of the agricultural resources of California than we had hitherto enjoyed. Soon after this, my brother left for distant mines.

CHAPTER XVIII

Now came a report to Marysville that rich diggings had been discovered at a place designated French Corral, which was about fifty miles from Marysville. This intelligence (as it ever does in California) caused hundreds of people, of all classes and professions, to rush simultaneously to the spot where gold was so gratuitously deposited. My husband was desirous of going too; and, possibly, he might establish a boarding-house there, if the prospect bid fair. So one morning, about a week after the tide of emigration had commenced flowing so rapidly, we started, and foolishly too, in a one-horse buggy. It was reported there was a good wagon-road leading directly to the place.

But what would be called a good wagon-road

there, would be considered utterly impassable here. Neither my husband nor myself had ever travelled in the mountains; if we had ever done so, no doubt we should have possessed wisdom enough to have taken the journey upon mules — decidedly the best mode of conveyance in the Sierra Nevada region. Early one morn in the month of June, we left the town of Marysville, long before the inhabitants had awakened from their drowsy slumbers, and pursued our course in a north-easterly direction, following the course of the Yuba, crossing and recrossing it several times during the day. About twenty miles from town, we struck the low hills (as they are termed) of the vast and gigantic Sierra Nevada range. Low hills! thought I. I should call them mountains, and higher ones, too, than I had ever dreamed of travelling over. Recollect, kind reader, I had been reared away down on Cape Cod, where there are only a few slight elevations, justly denominated sand-banks. After reaching the top of a high hill, (I suppose I must call it so, but it would suit my ideas better to say mountain,) the wheels were chained, preparatory to a descent. How my heart beat, and how I wished myself back again, before we reached the base! It was one of my pet horses that drew us, and I knew he was perfectly gentle; but oh, how I pitied him!

How entirely different was the scenery now from that enjoyed when traversing the beautiful valley of the Sacramento a short time previous! and yet in what close proximity these different sections lay! I could scarcely realize that I had not travelled thousands of miles, to reach a country so very dissimilar. After one becomes accustomed to mountain travel, I know not to which of these decidedly dissimilar landscapes the lover of nature would yield the palm. After overcoming in part the emotions of fear, I was perfectly entranced at beholding the lofty mountains towering far above us, their sides and summits timbered with large pines, firs, and cedars. And then how quiet and lovely looked those little valleys, so hidden and enclosed from the world, completely hemmed in by the grand and sublime elevations of nature's most magnificent handiwork! Oh, what dark and gloomy-looking defiles were disclosed to view! — fit rendezvous for the sanguinary assassin, or the dark-skinned treacherous savage. An involuntary shudder ran through my frame, as we wended our way through these silent mountain recesses.

I half-expected, every moment, to hear the whizzing of an Indian arrow past my ear, or the sharp click of the murderer's revolver. We were well armed, for it was dangerous to travel in those mountains unarmed. But I very much doubted my ability, so far as regarded courage, to use any weapon, (except woman's weapon,) even in self-defence. Often, as you enter one of these little valleys, your eyes will be greeted with the sight of a little shanty. Sometimes they call these mountain-glens corrals; and certainly they are corralled in by almost impervious barriers. One, in particular, arrested my attention. This valley was of an emerald green. Through it ran a clear, gurgling mountain-stream, the music of its waters inviting the weary wayfarer to sip of the health-promoting beverage. (I regret to add, at that time in California the health-inspiring properties of pure, unadulterated cold water were seldom tested.) Several cattle and mules were nibbling the green grass. But the prettiest feature of all, in my estimation, was an intelligent, bright-eyed little woman, seated just outside the door, under the shade of a magnolia, with a smiling, rosy little baby in her arms. I was out of the buggy in an instant, and had the little darling in my arms. There we obtained refreshments. There was quite a history connected with this bright-eyed woman, which I afterwards learned, and will relate, if my readers will pardon the episode. It may perhaps interest them as much in the recital as it did me.

We will now glance back through many years to the innocent days of childhood — to this lady's pleasant home on the banks of the lovely Connecticut. Not far from the shores of the Sound, which receives its limpid waters, stood a quaint, old-fashioned farm-house; and *there* she passed the spring-time of youth. On an adjacent farm dwelt another happy family. Not a day passed but the children of these respective families had met, and raced and tumbled about, in all the wild joy of freedom and of health; now paddling on the smooth surface of the glassy river, or scrambling among thorns and briers in those old woods, after violets and nuts, knowing no restraint, or recognizing none, save their parents' love. When she was about twelve years of age, her father conceived the idea of emigrating to the Western wilds.

Then those children, who had lived, and loved, and played together so long, must separate. The heroine of my story, and a lad a few years her senior, belonging to the other family, had, almost unconsciously, as it were, conceived and cherished an almost undying friendship for each other; the strength and ardor of which, the parents little suspected. After an interchange of many little love-tokens, the lad placed a hair ring, of curious workmanship, upon the girl's finger, with the solemn injunction never to part with it, and that, when he grew to be a man, he would seek her for his bride; and so they parted. Upon their arrival in the Western country, the father located himself, with his family, at or near Nauvoo city. Subsequently, he joined the Mormons, and resided many years at this place. About the time the tide of emigration commenced flowing to the golden shores of the Pacific, he put in execution the secretly cherished plan of removing with his family to Great Salt Lake city.

In vain our heroine — now grown to a lovely and interesting woman — sought to deter her father from consummating this long-cherished plan of removal to the city of Zion. We can conjecture how much she was influenced in adopting such a course by the knowledge which she had recently obtained that the lover of her youth, to whom she had, in defiance of oft-repeated solicitations to the contrary, ever proved faithful, was about to seek her for a fulfilment of his boyish pledge. Her father was inexorable : he was determined upon going, and his favorite daughter must accompany them. The mother's pleadings, too, could not be resisted. They started. The mother's health, previously enervated, after six weeks' toilsome travel across the plains, began visibly to decline. With intense anxiety, each succeeding day, they watched the paling cheek and tremulous motions of the wife and mother. Their worst fears were realized. One calm, still, moonlight eve, they consigned to a lonely grave the remains of the loved one. She had emigrated to her last peaceful home. Never more would she be called upon to resume her toilsome march across the plains of this sublunary sphere. The family now consisted of the widowed husband, the daughter, and a little girl, the offspring of a younger daughter, who had deceased several years previous to this last emigration, and, being a widow, had bequeathed her only child to its grand-parents. Little Rosa was a joyous, light-hearted child, possessed of strong affections. The rich wealth of love she had bestowed upon the grandmother had often caused the tears of that fond parent to flow at the thought of the bitter sorrow in store for the little darling, when she should have departed to her long home.

The grief of the child under this affliction was

deep and lasting. Never more was her sweet voice heard in unison with the feathered songsters, carolling her sweetest songs all the live-long day. Whenever they encamped, she would wander forth, and gather the prairie-roses, of which she begged her aunt to make for her a pillow. Upon this little pillow of roses every night she rested her tired head, covered with flaxen curls. One night, she complained of being unusually tired, and said, " Oh, aunty, where is my rosy pillow? That will cure me." In the morning, they found her in a raging fever, from which she never recovered. In two weeks from the time, she wept inconsolably at the grave of her grandmother; she had gone to join her in the spirit-land. They laid her in her little grave, with the pillow of roses under her head, and resumed their gloomy march.

In less than one week from this second bereavement, while fording a river, the father lost his life. Thus was the daughter left alone, the last of her family. She continued her journey with the company, and arrived safely at Salt Lake city. Here another trial awaited her. She had not been long there, before the great prophet, Brigham Young, selected her to swell the list of his spiritual wives, of whom at that time there were about thirty.

Her heart revolted at the idea of such a destiny, and she resolved upon speedy flight. A company of emigrants, bound to California, were encamped a short distance from the city. Thither she secretly directed her steps, told her story, was admitted into the company, and conveyed to California. Upon her arrival there, she was engaged as an assistant in a hotel, where she remained nearly a year.

One night, the occupants of this hotel were aroused by the appalling cry of "Fire!" in their midst. The building was in a blaze. Every one was rushing to obtain egress. At such a time, woe to those prostrated upon a bed of sickness! The shrieks of a sick man arrested the rapid steps of this woman, flying for safety from the devouring element. Many had rushed past, unmindful of his call for succor, intent only on self-preservation; but the kind heart of woman could not resist this touching appeal to her sympathies. She caught him in her arms, (for he was reduced to a mere skeleton, from intense suffering,) and rushed forth, just in time to escape the falling timbers. By the assistance of another person, the sick man was conveyed to comfortable quarters, where every attention was rendered him by the lady who had preserved his life on that eventful night. Owing to extreme excitement in his then weak state, a violent delirium ensued, which continued for many days. None knew the sufferer, or from whence he came. Upon his restoration to reason, as his kind nurse was proffering to him a glass of water, he suddenly sank back upon his pillow in a fainting fit. When consciousness was once more restored, he could only point to a hair ring upon the lady's finger, and articulate her name. Thus these lovers met, after a separation of nearly eighteen years. An explanation ensued, by which she learned that he had traced and followed her across the plains to Salt Lake city. There he lost all clue to her whereabouts. Disappointed and sick at heart, he pursued his way to California; went to the mines, and worked awhile, and was there taken sick. He managed to get to the hotel the day preceding the fire. The rest may be imagined by the situation in which I described her, as first seen by me upon entering that lovely valley. Truly, truth is stranger than fiction; and romance dwindles into insignificance, when contrasted with thrilling realities.

Now I will proceed on our journey. I regretted to leave that beautiful spot, so rural, so retired, so far from the busy haunts of man. It had such a serene aspect, it seemed to me to be one of the sweetest havens of rest that God ever provided for life's weary pilgrim. We travelled on until we reached another valley, equally as rich in nature's adornments; but its verdant soil had been recently saturated with the blood of three prospecting miners. Their bodies had been found pierced with arrows, besides being cut and mangled in a horrible manner. Some Indians near by were suspected of committing the murder. Consequently a number of miners had assembled, and, in order to intimidate the tribe, had taken three Indians, and hung them on the limb of a tree near by the scene of the murder. As we approached, we noticed with some anxiety the unusual collection of so many miners. Very soon the occasion of such an assemblage became apparent. There, on a single limb, were suspended the dead bodies of three Indians. One glimpse was sufficient. I can see them now, their swarthy, distorted visages emblematic of revenge and treachery.

Finally we came to a little mountain town called Bridgeport. It consisted of three little shanties and a toll-bridge, which spanned the Yuba River. The setting sun was just gilding the tops of the surrounding mountains, as we halted in front of one of the dwellings to inquire the distance to

French Corral. They informed us it was about five miles. They told us there was a pretty high mountain just beyond, and advised us to discontinue our journey for that night. They seemed so particularly solicitous for us to remain all night, their shanty was so filthily dirty, and they themselves were such savage, hirsute-looking objects, that I entreated my husband to go on. I thought, out of two evils, we were choosing the least by proceeding. I came to a different conclusion, however, before we reached our destination. My husband paid one dollar and a half toll, and we crossed a high bridge, under which rolled the Yuba. At this place, it was a rapidly rushing stream. It went foaming and dashing over innumerable rocks which intercepted its progress, overleaping every barrier, acknowledging no superior power. Unceasingly it rolled on its course, its waters mingling with those of her sister rivers, and *all* tending to one point, viz., the broad Pacific.

Directly after crossing the Yuba, we commenced the toilsome ascent of the highest mountain we had yet encountered. At the commencement of the ascent, my husband alighted to walk up the mountain, and I was to drive up. The poor horse started with all the energy he possessed, in the hope, I suppose, of speedily gaining the top. I quickly lost sight of my husband, who was trudging on in the vain hope of overtaking me. Soon I began to perceive evident signs of exhaustion in the horse. I tried to stop him, but could not. The buggy drew back so, that, if he attempted to stop, it drew him back too. And oh, what an awful road it was! Deep gullies worn by streams of water, which had flowed down when the snow had melted, deep enough to hide myself in! I tried several times to get the carriage crosswise the road, but could not, on account of those gullies and huge rocks.

I was fearful, every moment, the horse would fall, from utter exhaustion. He was covered with white foam, and his tongue was extended from his mouth. I screamed for my husband at the top of my voice; but he was puffing and blowing far down the mountain. I finally contrived to get the carriage wedged in between two rocks. I then got out, and went to the relief of the horse. Poor fellow! I thought he was dying, for some time. When my husband appeared in sight, his appearance betokened about as great exhaustion as the horse. After a good rest, we all proceeded up, I on foot too. Three or four times I threw myself on the ground in utter exhaustion. We could not proceed as leisurely as we would, had night not been so close upon us. The summit was reached; and what a magnificent view greeted my wondering vision! The road wound round the mountain near the top. The sides of the mountain had been cut down, and a very good level road formed, of just sufficient width for only one carriage to pass round at a time. A horn, which is found at each termination of this narrow pass, is loudly sounded by travellers, before entering on the road, as a warning of their approach. The distance from this road down an almost perpendicular descent was one thousand feet; and at the base of the mountain rolled the foaming waters of the Yuba River. Yet from that dizzy height it had the appearance of a white ribbon no wider than your hand. The outside wheels of the buggy ran within three feet of the edge of the precipice. Nothing could induce me to ride (even with our gentle horse) in such close proximity to the frightful chasm. My husband jumped in and rode around, while I went plodding along, almost ankle-deep in the red sand. Presently I heard voices behind. I turned to look, and there, a few paces behind me, were two dark, swarthy, bewhiskered individuals, each mounted on a fine mule, and one of them was leading a spare mule. What to do I did not know. There I was, alone, wallowing in the sand, my bonnet off, hair dishevelled, face the color of vermilion, and dress the color of the sand. Who or what I was, or how I came there on foot, I suppose was beyond their comprehension.

When they overtook me, one said, "Good evening, madam; this is a hard road to travel over Jordan." To this I made no reply. Said the other, "Wont you ride? you look tired." I told him there was a carriage waiting for me just round the mountain. So they rode on. Soon I found my husband waiting for me. I quickly accepted his invitation to ride, for I feared meeting with other adventures, which might not terminate so pleasantly. We travelled on, expecting to reach the corral every moment. There were no more such high elevations on our route as the last we had surmounted; but there were a plenty high enough, I assure you.

But for the brilliant rays of the queen of night, we should have been compelled to encamp in the mountains. Nothing could exceed the grandeur and sublimity of these mountain-glens and cañons, walled in by those grand and lofty mountains, and lighted by the brilliant and powerful rays of the moon, and the sparkling radiance of the starry host, glittering like so many diamonds in the deep-blue canopy of the heavens. Their desolation is mellowed; an air of purity and holiness seems to pervade those silent places, which leads the imagination to picture them as grand saloons of nature, fashioned by the hand of the Almighty for the residence of pure and uncontaminating substances, and not for the doomed children of passion, want, care, and sorrow.

About ten in the evening, we made our descent into the valley bearing the name of French Corral. We were perfectly astonished at beholding such a collection of canvas houses — large frame boarding-houses and hotels, brilliantly lighted gambling-saloons without number, and Spanish dance-houses, French cafés, drinking-saloons, etc., etc.

It may not be amiss to state here the manner of building frame-houses, when the time occupied in building was two days for a private dwelling, four days for a hotel, and six days for a church. The last mentioned, however, was not often raised. A building would boast of a very slight frame, not boarded, but split clapboard nailed on to the frame, and the outside was finished. Upon the inside, in lieu of laths and plastering, bleached or unbleached. cotton cloth is stretched smoothly and tightly, and fastened to the frame. This cloth is then papered over, and it looks as nice as paper upon plastering. The ceiling overhead is nice bleached cloth, sewed together neatly, and stretched so tightly there is not a wrinkle observable. For partitions a frame is raised, and each side of this frame is cloth and paper, leaving a hollow space between the two partitions of cloth, about three or four inches in width. These partitions look as firm and solid as they do made the usual way; but they afford but a slight hindrance to the passage of sounds. These deceptive partitions have been accessory to the diffusion of many a momentous secret.

Begging pardon for this digression, I will proceed with the description of this speedily-rushed-into-existence mining town. We were directed to the California Hotel, as one capable of rendering the best accommodations. Thither we accordingly went, and received a hearty reception. Every attention benighted, tired travellers could reasonably require, was cheerfully conferred. Next morning, we rose from our couches of straw, rather lame, to be sure, but anxious, nevertheless, to reconnoitre the town. We first repaired to the mines. There were over one thousand miners at work in a gulch surrounded by towering mountains, which shot up almost perpendicularly over their heads. The frosts of spring tarry latest in those gulches, and the genial rays of the winter sun penetrate but occasionally to cheer the miner in his arduous toil.

It is difficult, after all the descriptions he may read, for any one who has not been in the mines to obtain any correct idea of the manner in which they are worked, or of the difficulties and singular vicissitudes in life to which the miner is exposed. If the miner be dependent upon others for his water by paying for it weekly, success demands that he should be an early riser. Before the first dawn of light breaks upon the sky above him, he opens his eyes, rolls over on his hard bed, stretches his stiffened limbs, and, feeling about for his boots, places his hand upon something resembling an icicle, into which his feet are thrust, and the labors of the day commenced. He kindles his fire, (that is, if he boards himself,) fills and sets on the coffee-pot, fries his "flap-jacks" and his pork, or warms up his beans, and the morning repast is prepared. It is then quickly eaten; and, by the time it is daylight, the miner is beside his tom. The water is let on, and in half an hour's time he is standing ankle-deep in it, while, every few minutes, a dash of it is accidentally sprinkled upon his back. A hard day's work of this kind is not unfrequently closed by the paltry reward of one, two, or three dollars, to be divided between the last named number of men. And this approximates, more nearly than all other histories, to the truth of mining. The "big strikes" are always heard of first, because the good news is published, while the bad is deemed worthy of no such distinction. From this cause thousands of people meet with disappointment, and write back to their Atlantic friends, reviling a country the noblest for its climate, soil, and business advantages, of any under the broad canopy of heaven.

The success of the miner depends a great deal upon luck. He may be industrious, economical, possessed of good morals, labor perseveringly for months, and sometimes years, and still be poor, as far as the acquisition of gold is concerned; while, perhaps, an unprincipled spendthrift in a few months may realize a fortune. A claim, too, may prospect rich, and yet, upon working it, yield scarcely sufficient to defray the expenses. Sometimes, also, adjoining claims which prospect alike may prove, one rich, and the other poor. I knew one fellow who had worked three weeks upon his claim, and had not realized enough to pay his board. He became disheartened, and sold out to a "green-horn," who, in the interval of six weeks, took out over three thousand dollars' worth of the yellow metal. I knew another, too, who labored hard three years in the country, without any more than defraying his expenses, when he was fortunate enough to strike a "pocket," from which he took out twenty thousand dollars. But here I am digressing again.

We found, upon walking about the town, that nearly every other building was a boarding-house. So much competition had reduced board to twelve dollars per week, which would not pay, considering the fact of having to pay six cents per pound freight for the transportation of provisions from Marysville; so my husband relinquished the idea of opening a house there, and decided to return to Marysville on the following day. That night, there was to be a grand ball at the Corral; and Mrs. R——, the wife of the gentleman who kept the house where we stopped, was very anxious for me to accompany her to witness the proceedings. Accordingly, in the course of the evening, we stepped in, as silent spectators of the festive scene. I was rather surprised at beholding such a recherché assemblage. By the appearance of the company, I should not have suspected that we were, figuratively speaking, in the bowels of the Sierra Nevada Mountains. A long artificial bower had been constructed, under which were spread the tables, loaded with delicious viands. There were turkeys, which at that period could not be purchased for less than twenty-five dollars apiece; and pigs, too, which were equally as scarce in the market. There were jellies and East India preserves temptingly displayed, also the refreshing ice-cream. Beautiful bouquets graced the tables. These flowers had been gathered in close proximity to snow. Sixteen miles distant, farther up in the mountains, was plenty of ice then; and there was a Frenchman at the Corral — from whom the place derived its name — who kept quite a number of cows; so that ice and cream were very easily obtained.

Here, fifty miles from the settlements, were convened a collection of gentlemen and ladies, who had come, some ten, some twenty, and some thirty miles, to join in the merry dance. I saw two Bostonians there. It was a select company: all gamblers were excluded.

After having regaled ourselves with some refreshments, which the polite and gentlemanly host insisted upon our partaking, we took our leave, as, the ensuing morning early, we were to start on our homeward journey.

It is a peculiar feature of the climate in California, that, as soon as the snow disappears from the earth, the flowers spring up spontaneously. There is no frost in the ground, and the heavy body of snow lying thereon serves to keep it warm. While at the Corral, I was presented with an elegant bouquet, which a gentleman told me he gathered between two snow-banks, in such close proximity to each other, that, with his arms extended, he could reach the snow on either side. The rising sun, next morning, found us at the top of that high mountain, very near the spot where he bade us adieu on our journey up.

Neither ourselves nor the horse were as fatigued as when we made the ascent; therefore, it did not appear half as formidable; yet I preferred being upon my feet. It was really frightful to look at the horse and buggy. The wheels were both chained: yet how the poor horse had to brace his feet at every step! It was on this same mountain, the following August, as a party of emigrants, who travelled across the plains, were descending in an ox-team, the wagon pitch-poled, distributing the contents (which consisted of a woman and two or three children, cooking-stove, and many other household utensils) in every direction.

When we reached Bridgeport, we were accosted by the toll-gatherer with "Well, I reckon as how you had a right smart heap of trouble that night, afore you reached the top of the mountain. I allowed you would be for turning back; but I have always heard say, them Yankee women never would give up beat." How he knew I was a Yankee, was beyond my comprehension; for he did not hear me speak, as I recollect of. Must be my countenance was the index of the nation to which I belonged; and I believe it does speak Yankee as well as my tongue; for I was never taken for anything else, except once ——.

We met with no adventure particularly worth relating on our homeward journey. When we descended again to the foot of the hills, they really seemed clipped of nearly one-half their altitude since I had passed over them. I was also surprised at the wonderful amount of courage I had acquired during the trip. Now I laughed at travelling over those hills I before had cried at. That night, the little canvas house received within its walls a tired couple. Not long after this did it afford us a home. My husband sold it, and we went to the Tremont Hotel, where I remained during the remainder of my stay in Marysville.

CHAPTER XIX.

Soon after this, I took a journey, in company with several ladies and gentlemen from San Francisco, to a mining locality, called Park's Bar, situated about twenty miles from Marysville. After leaving the plain, our route lay through a thick growth of what is there termed chaparell. It resembles, at a distance, the hawthorn. So dense is this growth of bushes, it affords grand lurking-places for the assassin. Many a poor miner, as he has trudged along, with his blankets upon his back, perhaps well laden with the shining dust, has at this place been pounced upon, and relieved of his burden, and perhaps his life, by some one of the many desperadoes who infest the country.

A gentleman of the company related an incident which occurred, as a friend of his was once travelling this particular locality. He was driving a mule-team very leisurely along, in close communion with his thoughts, when, all at once, he was startled from his reverie by the sudden halting of his mules. Upon looking up, there, close in advance of the mules, were two huge grisly bears, amusing themselves with their cubs. His heart was in his mouth in an instant. How could he compete with two such formidable antagonists, should they simultaneously attack him? His mules betrayed the terror they were suffering by one long, continuous bray, in which they were speedily joined by their no less frightened driver. This horrid din, suddenly bursting upon this bruin coterie, had the desired effect. They instantly disappeared in the surrounding chaparell; while the teamster pursued his way with all possible dispatch, congratulating himself upon having escaped, at least, a very *feeling* embrace. While speaking of this graminivorous animal, allow me to add, that I was acquainted with a family who had in their possession a cub, so tame that he used to play about the floor with the children as harmlessly as a pet-kitten. He was prized so highly, they had declined several tempting offers to part with him. Some hunters had shot his mother, and were dragging her off, when this little cub ran after them, sprang upon its dead mother, and evinced the strongest symptoms of affection. Thus it was easily captured.

About mid-day, we arrived at our destination — quite a little town, picturesquely situated upon the banks of the Yuba. Those little mountain towns are, to me, invested with a charm, a novelty, that is perfectly bewitching. After refreshing ourselves at a hotel in the vicinity, we repaired to the mining ground, as we laughingly remarked, to prospect. Some of the miners were so very gallant as to offer us the use of their pans, at the same time assuring us that they would allow us all the gold dust we were lucky enough to pan out. It was considered rich diggins at this spot; therefore, the vision of a heap of gold dust incited us at once to doff our lace sleeves and fancy fixings, and enter zealously upon this to us novel method of obtaining that coveted metal. Oh, it was back-aching work, I assure you!

Since that one half hour's work in the mines, how much sympathy I have felt for the gold-diggers! The thought at once obtruded itself, that if some of the wives of these poor miners whom I had known could but realize one half of the toil and hardships their husbands endure in the acquisition of wealth, or of even a competency, by the use of the pan and shovel, they would not be half so lavish in their expenditures. It was excessively warm; there was not a breath of air stirring; the sun was shining down with more than tropical fervor, while its rays were reflected in ten thousand directions from the sides of the hills, until the atmosphere glowed and glimmered like the air in a furnace.

Although the earth was yielding at the rate of ten cents to the panful, we very soon came to the conclusion, that we had rather suffer the privations incident to poverty than toil longer in that burning heat; so, wiping the perspiration from our vermilion countenances, we repaired to the hotel; from whence, after a short rest, I sallied forth to visit several female acquaintances of mine who resided at the Bar. They were ladies who, upon their first arrival in the country, had boarded with us awhile, until their husbands could provide a suitable abode for them in the mines.

I found one of them, a Mrs. Q——, suffering excessively from a terrible fright she had received the night previous. The facts were these: They kept a boarding-house, where they accommodated about forty persons. In the night, they were both awakened by a noise in their room. Before they could move, and even before her husband could grasp a revolver which lay loaded under his pillow, the figure of a man, masked, and holding a sharp, glittering knife in his hand, was standing over them. The knife was held within an inch of her throat, while the threat was uttered, that if her husband moved so much as an inch, his wife's life would pay the penalty. Such a threat was, of course, effective. There they lay, while three other burglars entered the room, and commenced pilfering. A trunk was opened, from whence they abstracted one thousand dollars in gold dust. Next followed her jewelry, and her gold watch, a parting present from her mother. Her husband's watch, and several other articles of value, was seized upon; with all of which they decamped. The sentinel still stood over the wife, while she had fainted from fright. After waiting until his co-workers in villany were fairly off, he told him, if he raised the alarm until the lapse of so many minutes after his departure, that a ball, from an unseen and unerring hand, would be the forfeiture. He then vamosed. The alarm, however, was instantly given; every inmate in the house were aroused; but no trace of the robbers was ever discovered. It was weeks, and even months, before Mrs. Q—— recovered from the shock she that night received.

I felt in hopes the party would conclude to

remain over night at the bar; but, as there was a bright moon, they decided upon a moonlight drive to Marysville. I must confess myself so much of a coward that I liked not to travel through those gloomy-looking cañons and ravines at night, even were the way illumined by brilliant Luna's beams. I fancied the shadows of the trees assumed the form of the lurking assassin, ready for a spring. We met with no adventure on the way home, and our ears were assailed with no more horrible sounds than the bark of the cayotes that prowled along on our track. These animals partake of the nature of the wolf, and are very cowardly. They are a great pest in California. The burial-ground, situated about a mile from Marysville, was often frequented by these animals; bodies were often found exhumed and partially devoured by them.

During my residence in California, situated as I was most of the time in a hotel, I had ample opportunity to study human nature in all its varied phases. Scenes of misery, too, I witnessed, enough to fill a volume, were they all recorded. Scenes of gayety and splendor also diversified the way. I attended one wedding in Marysville, the cost of which was currently estimated at two thousand dollars. The bride was a fair widow of thirty, (and wealthy withal,) whose husband had deceased five months previously.

People in our staid, matter-of-fact, puritanical towns, can have but a faint conception of the ever-varying, ever-changing scenes, pertaining to a life in California, where fortunes are made and lost in a day; friends die, and are forgotten soon, in the constant whirl of excitement which surrounds one. People who, when I first arrived in California, were considered immensely rich in this world's goods, long before I left were reduced to penury. The motto there is, "Nothing risked, nothing gained." They will perhaps invest all they possess in some great speculation, (always bound to succeed,) and lose the whole. Then, again, vice versa.

What shocked me more than all else in California was, to see the poor, sick, and often penniless people, brought to the hotels (there were no hospitals in Marysville at that time) to die; and then, when the soul had taken its flight to the spirit-land, to see the hearse drive to the door, take the body, which had been deposited in a rough box without the usual apparelling for the grave, and start off to the place of interment alone! Not one solitary mourner to follow the remains, or drop the tear of affection at the grave of one who, perhaps, in some far-distant home, had many "loving friends, and true," who were anxiously waiting and watching for his return.

One day there were two brothers, brought by their father to the Tremont Hotel. They were sick with a fever. After a week of intense suffering, they died, and the lone father followed them to their last resting-place. A few days subsequent to this event, he was attacked with the same fever which had proved fatal to his sons. He soon felt convinced that he, too, must die. When the proprietor of the house asked him if he had friends in the Atlantic states, to whom he wished word to be conveyed, "No," said he; "I am the last of my race. I have no friend living to mourn for me." He even declined naming the place of his birth. In a few days after that, he lay beside his boys.

At another time, the mangled form of a young and intelligent-looking man was brought to a hotel. He had been crushed in a horrible manner by the falling of a large rock where he was at work. His head and chest alone remained uninjured. A younger brother accompanied him to the hotel, and remained as his nurse. Every night he used to slip quietly from his suffering brother's room, and repair to the gambling-houses, and there stake and lose large sums, which had been obtained at the price of his brother's life. The poor sick man, unable to raise a finger, his back turned towards the door, and therefore not knowing his brother was absent, would call repeatedly the brother's name, begging him for a glass of water. After a while, all would be still. No one suspected he was dying there alone nights.

One night, I heard the call so long continued, and so plaintively uttered, I could endure it no longer. I rose, dressed myself, and repaired to the sufferer's room. I found him all alone. "I wish, madam," he said, "you would waken Jack. He sleeps so soundly, I never can arouse him in the night. I call until I am fearful of awakening the occupants of the surrounding rooms, and then I desist. But now I think I am dying." I told him his brother's bed was vacant. He seemed very much distressed at his brother's absence. Search was immediately instituted. He was found at a gambling-table, betting. He was summoned to the bedside of his brother. After a while, the sick man revived. He lingered through the next day. At night, his physician enjoined his brother to remain constantly with him, as it was not probable he would survive until morning. The passion for gambling had gained such an ascendency over the young brother's better feelings, that, some time during the silent watches of the night, he had deserted his dying brother! In the morning, the poor sufferer was found a corpse. He had died alone! What struggles, what agonizing thoughts, were his, what words passed his dying lips, none save his Maker knew.

The brother had passed the night in one of the many dens of infamy that abounded, and which shed, and still do, a withering blight over the fair and sunny valleys of the richest country the sun ever shone upon. See, in this case, what a pernicious influence those gilded saloons of vice have upon the unstable mind of youth. Here were two brothers, who had been reared by fond parents in the fear and admonition of the Lord. Through their childhood they had loved one another; and together they had repaired to a distant land to seek their fortunes. The younger, whose mind was more vacillating, had by degrees yielded to the song of that siren, Vice, until she had lured him to her haunts, causing him to forget home, friends, and even a dying brother, to follow in the train of the tempter.

My prayers are, and ever have been, with the

vigilance committees of California. May the blessing of God attend them, and prosper all their undertakings and endeavors to uproot and exterminate those hot-beds of vice, those quick-sands in the ocean of life, upon which the bark of many a promising youth, of many a young husband, and of many a middle-aged father, has been irrecoverably wrecked.

Go into the villages and towns throughout the Atlantic States, and in how many will you not find one, at least, who has been a heart-sufferer from the effects of those dens of sin and iniquity, which, until the organization of the vigilance committee, threw open their gilded doors, even in the glare of noon-day, to allure the weak-minded and unsuspecting! And even the strong-minded have sometimes fallen a prey to their seductive wiles. How many homes have been rendered desolate, how many families disunited and severed, how many hearts as well as fortunes broken, by the prevalence of that one great sin, gambling! and it has been an almost universal vice in California.

How many enterprising and ambitious men have I known who emigrated with their happy wives to California, their hearts buoyant with bright anticipations of the future! Success for awhile crowned all their undertakings; but, alas! those gorgeously furnished drinking-saloons which meet the eye at every turn proved too enticing for frail human nature to resist. The first temptation yielded to, and how easily the downward course is pursued, which terminates in total depravity!

The young wife, neglected by her husband, her brilliant hopes crushed, — unless she be possessed of a strong mind, and has friends there to guide and guard her, — rather than return alone to the home of her childhood, gradually loses her self-respect, and finally swells the list of those we blush to name.

Those upon whom the sun of prosperity has ever shone, know not how bitterly painful is the first clouding over of youth's sweet visions — the first crushing blight of confidence and love — the first consciousness that life is not so fair and bright, nor friends so kind and true, as we have pictured them. Not from observation wholly do I asseverate these statements — by sad experience have these sentiments become deeply imbedded in my heart. I have known, and felt, and suffered *all*, in my short life. But, when the wife's cup of misery is full to overflowing, and she returns to the home of her youth, expecting to receive the sympathy she so justly deserves, and which is so readily proffered by those encircling her own hearth-stone, how poignant to her sensitive and lacerated feelings are the baneful, whispered slanders which are borne to her ears! and emanating, too, from the lips of those she once considered friends, and who, had adversity not overtaken her, would still have been fawning sycophants for favor.

Oh, ye slanderers! pause in your career; for it is one of the most heinous sins that the instigator of all evil ever conceived, and from which every pure heart will turn with loathing and disgust. If the professed slanderer ever has any moments of serious reflection, how severe must be the accusations of that faithful monitor within; for to how many, in the course of their life-time, have they cast their poisoned arrows, dipped in the foul extract of their own hearts, which, while it *kills* not those to whom it is aimed, rankles deeply in a sensitive heart, causing tears of agony to flow! Then there are always plenty of the lovers of gossip abroad to catch and retail slander; plenty ready to believe an evil report, without taking the trouble to investigate. Thus many an innocent heart has palpitated keenly, upon receiving manifest slights from a source whence they had a right to expect nought but kindness.

CHAPTER XX.

ONE bright morning, toward the latter part of the month of September, I left Marysville for a drive to General Sutter's residence, situated about eight miles below Marysville. You cross Feather River at Yuba city, and follow the banks of this lovely stream, the scene varied and beautified by nature's incomparable adornments, until the picturesque mansion of the affable and dignified general greets the eye. The road leads to the back entrance of the spacious, square court-yard, which is surrounded by a range of buildings on three sides. Several large and stately trees rear their umbrageous branches far above the roofs of the adobe buildings, which, from their sylvan retreat, peep out a ready welcome to the tired stranger. The grounds around the dwelling are tastefully and beautifully adorned with numerous parterres, some of which are inclosed with hedges of cactus. Here I saw the first cultivated rose that had greeted my eye since leaving New England. How the sight of those roses carried me back to the neat New England homes, embowered with honey-suckle and roses! It was actually fragrant with home, and home associations. On one side of the gardens extended a flourishing vineyard, the products of which amply repaid the labor expended thereon.

We were invited by the general to enter his pleasant-looking domicile, which invitation we cheerfully accepted. We were regaled with grapes, as luscious, I dare say, as the forbidden fruit which tempted the occupants of paradise. The wines proffered, — the produce of the vines of California, — having attained age, were pronounced of an excellent quality in substance and flavor. Sweet music, discoursed by one of the general's sons, enhanced the pleasure of this often-remembered visit.

The Indians in the immediate vicinity are devoted to the general's service; while the only remuneration they ask or expect is their food. His house servants are all the female Diggers. The general's family carriage is drawn by two sleek-looking mules; and the driver's box is occupied by a Digger Indian, in costume à la fancy. Mrs. Sutter generally denies herself to all visitors; but the regret generated by her absence speedily vanishes in the presence of the affable, courteous general, who ever welcomes his visitors with a cordiality inseparable from the man, whose integrity never bent to wrong or pusillanimous expediency, and who, armed intellectually with the panoply of justice, has courage to sustain it, under all and any circumstances.

We arrived back to Marysville just as the red orb of day touched the rim of the western horizon, covering it all with crimson and gold, and filling the world with a flood of evening glory.

I was often amused, while sojourning at the Tremont, by witnessing the transformations effected by a change of apparel on the inhabitants of the mountains, when they made temporary visits to the valleys. One day, a weary and care-worn-looking miner entered the bar-room of the hotel. Nought of his countenance was visible save his eyes and nose; for over his brow was drawn a soiled Kossuth hat; while the lower part of his face was entirely concealed by an abundant growth of hair. He deposited his blankets upon the floor, advanced to the bar-keeper, and inquired for the proprietor of the house. To him this soiled and travelled-stained miner delivered up thousands for safe keeping. He seated himself in the gentlemen's parlor, eyeing intently for some moments an open piano. Upon his advancing toward it, and seating himself upon the music-stool, a smile, bordering on derision, involuntarily passed from one to another of the occupants of the room. The smile, however, was speedily changed to looks of astonishment, when, after running his fingers hastily over the keys, music such as we sometimes hear in our dreams, but *very* seldom in every-day life, gushed upon their astonished senses. The air was "Sweet Home." He accompanied the instrument with a voice of surpassing melody, which penetrated to the ladies' rooms, and brought them en masse to the stairs, where they remained almost spell-bound, while he played and sang piece after piece, seemingly engrossed by heart-awakening memories of other days and other lands, and wholly unconscious of the presence of listeners who had gathered around him. As he was about midway in the execution of that plaintive song, "Katy Darling," he suddenly ceased, became aware of the attention he was attracting, caught up his old, greasy hat, and vamosed.

When next he appeared in their midst, the metamorphosis was so complete as to utterly prevent recognition, had he not again seated himself at the piano. He remained several weeks at the hotel, and often delighted us with specimens of his musical talent. He was considered by connoisseurs as the greatest performer upon the piano in all California.

I never saw a miner without thinking how little

one could judge, by the present appearance, of his origin or past life, for there were those laboring in the gold mines of California who had held important offices of trust in the Atlantic states. The sons of wealthy southern planters, too, were there, laboring as hard as their fathers' slaves at home, but reaping a far richer harvest of gold. People who at home never performed any manual labor, there would not hesitate to stand in water up to their knees for days and weeks together, if, by so doing, they could heap high their coffers.

The good fortune of a lady in California, which came under my especial observation, I will here record. Upon the arrival at Marysville of one of the up-river boats, a fine-looking lady, whose age might perhaps be thirty or thereabouts, came to the Tremont Hotel, and desired an interview with the proprietor. She informed him she was entirely destitute of funds, as the journey from New York had been more expensive than she had expected, and begged, as a favor, the loan of twenty dollars. Could she obtain that amount, she intended to pursue her way to Downieville, where she hoped and expected to find a friend and relative. The proprietor accordingly proffered the required sum, although somewhat doubtful of receiving it again, or even of seeing the recipient. The next morning she resumed her journey; and the remembrance of this fine-looking widow was obliterated by the occurrence of other and more important affairs. Five or six weeks had elapsed, when, one day, she astonished us all by appearing in our midst. Upon meeting the proprietor, "Oh," said she, "I have been *so* successful! and now I have come to liquidate old debts." The nature of the success was this: She arrived at Downieville, found the one of whom she was in pursuit, and he built her a canvas house, procured her a cooking-stove, a long board table, and some wooden benches, and she commenced keeping a boarding-house. She soon had thirty or forty boarders, for each of which she received twelve dollars per week. One day, as she was sweeping her floor, — which, by the way, was nothing but the earth, — she saw something glitter. Upon examination, it proved to be a lump of gold. She searched farther, and found the earth was full of particles of gold. She instantly summoned to her presence the friend who had assisted her in locating herself in such rich diggings. They removed the table, benches, and stove. Upon the last-named utensil a dinner was in progress; but who would think of preparing a dinner, even if it were near the dinner hour, should they suddenly find themselves in possession of such rich diggings. This land, which she had appropriated to her own use, was situated in a central part of the town of Downieville. It had never been prospected, for the very reason that its appearance betokened nought to impress the beholder with the idea that gold existed there in such quantities.

That day they two took from the kitchen floor, as she termed it, five hundred dollars, mostly in lumps. Every day witnessed similar success. As soon as she could think of leaving her treasures for two days, she hastened to Marysville to cancel her debts. Afterwards she became a frequent visitor at the house. I became very well acquainted with her; and one day she related the cause of her leaving home alone, to seek a home in California. She was married very young, and in opposition to the wishes of her parents. Unfortunately, her married life proved miserable in the extreme. After a lapse of years, she returned penniless, with one child, to the home of her youth, where she received a hearty welcome from her father; but the gentle, loving mother, whom she had forsaken, had gone long since to the spirit-land, and her place in the family circle was occupied by another. That other regretted the daughter's return, and manifested her disapproval by unkindness to the child. At one time, when the child was suffering intensely from sickness, child-like he refused to take his medicine, whereupon the grandmother struck him. In twenty-four hours after that, the boy was a corpse. After the burial of her boy, the daughter never looked upon the step-mother again. She told her father, that, if he would furnish her with means, she would seek her fortune in California; and she did, in the manner above related. She acquired a fortune; but the recollection of her boy, at times, would come floating over the ocean of memory, overshadowing all the bright hopes and sunny feelings of her heart.

It was a novel sight to me to watch the emigrant wagons, as they passed through Marysville to their different destinations. How dusty and travel-stained they appeared, after a four and five months' journey across those almost boundless prairies, after fording those mighty streams, whose waters had been navigated by nought save the red man's canoe, effecting a passage through lonely cañons and over towering mountains, 'enduring almost every hardship the human frame is capable of sustaining, and finally had reached the desired goal!

How emaciated the cattle looked; and no wonder, for how many long and weary miles they had travelled! I almost fancied those old oxen actually smiled for joy at arriving at their destination; yet many of their number had given out on the way, and their bones lay bleaching in the sun.

A lady who had travelled across the plains told me how sad it made her feel when she saw the cattle giving out on the way. Said she, "Those dumb beasts would express so much sorrow in their faces when they began to falter in their pace, they would look so wishfully into the face of the teamster, and low so mournfully, I knew they understood their situation."

Notwithstanding the sufferings and hardships those emigrants endure while on their "winding way," all is forgotten when they reach the settlements. Their swarthy, sun-burned faces are radiant with joy as they pass along.

It is astonishing how much one of those wagons will hold. I saw one passing with eight holes cut in the canvas on one side, and a child's face peeping out at every one of these holes. Besides the children it contained, there were cats, dogs, beds and bedding, cooking-stove, tin pans, and kettles.

Two emigrant wagons passed through town one day, each driven by two beautiful-looking girls — beautiful, although browned by exposure to the weather. In their hands they carried one of those tremendous, long ox-whips, which, by great exertion, they flourished, to the evident admiration of all beholders. Their surpassing beauty gained for them the appellation of the "belles of the plains." In two weeks from the time they attracted so much attention, driving each three yoke of oxen through town, they were married to gentlemen whom they had never seen until they arrived in California, and who had never seen them until they beheld them as teamsters.

I often saw ladies at the hotel who had resided eight and twelve months at different bars far up in the mountains, where they were the only females, and during all this time would not see a lady to speak to. You can imagine how fast they would talk, upon getting where there were plenty of their own sex.

I was quite amused at an incident related by one of those ladies, who had been for eight months thus isolated from all society. Her husband kept a boarding-house, where he accommodated about thirty miners, which were all that worked at that place. A short time previous to the occurrence of the scene here related, these miners had had some trouble with a tribe of Indians whose rancheria was not far distant. They had heard several times that they meditated an attack upon all the whites in their vicinity, and for some time they had been upon their guard; but, as they heard nothing from them, they had relaxed their watchfulness. One day, when they were all at work in the mines, and this lady alone in the house, instantaneously a deafening war-whoop rang in her ears. She ran to the door, and saw, at a little distance from the house, about two hundred painted Indians, armed with bows, arrows, and hatchets, advancing at a rapid pace. She rushed from the house, frightened half to death, (as she expressed her feelings,) and ran, screaming, to the spot where the men were at work. They, hearing the war-whoop and her screams, and seeing the whole tribe making such a rapid descent, naturally supposed they were coming to exterminate them; and if so, flight was out of the question. There was no alternative but to meet the foe, and fight with picks and shovels; for their fire-arms were in the house, and the Indians were between the house and where they were. They directed Mrs. —— to flee across the river and into the woods on the opposite side, and secrete herself as quickly as possible. The river was so deep, the water so wild and dark-looking, and spanned by so narrow a timber, that, upon any ordinary occasion, she would have hesitated a long time before venturing across; but now, with the velocity of the wind almost, she crossed the timber, and rushed with headlong speed for the woods. Before reaching it, however, she passed several large excavations in the earth; and, thinking one of these would afford her a grand hiding-place, she jumped into it, and crouched down to await her fate. Said she, "It would be impossible to describe my feelings while in this hole. I expected every moment to see a dozen dark-skinned savages, glaring at me with their murderous, blood-thirsty eyes. I could endure it no longer: I must crawl out, and rush on. After great exertion, I got out, and, not once daring to look around, made all haste for the woods.

"Reaching it, I would hide myself for a few moments, and then think, 'They will surely find me here; I must find a better place than this;' and then leave it in search of another. In this way I hid myself a dozen times. Finally, I climbed up into the branches of a large tree, and there remained, for how long I could not tell — the time seemed interminable. Then I heard some one shouting. I was so terrified, I could scarcely retain my seat. Soon I heard my own name called, and recognized my husband's voice. *He* was alive, then, and all the others were murdered! When he appeared in sight, he was laughing. I thought him insane. Said he, "Come down from the tree; it is all right. I thought I should never find you. I have been hunting these two hours.'"

It seemed these Indians had started, in honor of some great occasion, to visit a neighboring tribe. They had painted and armed themselves, as they ever do when they start upon a journey to celebrate any great event. Their object in raising such a war-whoop was, doubtless, a sportive one; for they passed the miners with their countenances illumined with a broad grin.

The lady, who was from the New England States, returned to her house with some idea of the sufferings of the early New England settlers. It was days before she recovered her usual equanimity.

Another lady told me that she was the first who arrived at Cañon Creek, situated a hundred miles from Marysville, in the Sierra Nevada Mountains; and that, when she arrived at the top of the mountain which overlooked the ravine in which the miners were at work, they desisted from their labors, gave three hearty cheers, and came to the place where she was seated on a mule. Their delight was so great at seeing a live woman in their midst, that they actually lifted the mule upon which she was riding from his feet, and carried them both down the mountain. Those miners, who had lived so long in their little cabins, secluded from the world, deprived of the cheering presence of woman, knew then, if they had never before known, how to appreciate the opposite sex.

As a specimen of the sort of accommodations a traveller is likely to meet with in a journey through the more unsettled parts of the mountains, I will describe a public-house on the trail (as it was called) that I once had occasion to stop at. It was a little log shanty, kept by a woman — of what color I was unable to determine, on account of the dirt upon her person. She hailed from out West, somewhere. I think it must have been far West, where the cleansing properties of soap and water were not often tested. There was no floor in this shanty but the earth, and even that looked as if it had never been swept. How could I stay, and eat, and sleep in so much dirt? There was no alternative; night was close at hand, and no other *public-house* within many miles. She prepared us a *good supper*, as she termed it, in which, I presume, there was a good supply of dirt, although I did not stop to scrutinize it very closely. After we had partaken of the cheer set before us, she washed the dishes, turned round, and dashed the dish-water up in one corner of the apartment, wiped her hands upon her dirty apology for a dress, and sat down for a smoke. For sleeping accommodations, there were berths built up against the side of this shanty. I wrapped my own blankets around me, and crawled into one of them, where I remained until daylight. Right glad was I when it appeared, and I hoped to leave her domicile without being encumbered with any of her live stock; but in this I was disappointed.

At one time there came down from the mountains the most comical-looking old couple I ever beheld. They were English, and had emigrated to the Western States ten years previous to the date of my story. They had been in California two years, during which time they had never left the mines. She worked mining with her husband. It was the commencement of the rainy season when they left the mines; and all she had on, to protect her from the weather, was a thin, faded calico gown — one which she had brought from

England ten years before; and it was the best garment she possessed. Over her shoulders she wore a calico jacket, and on her head an apology for a sun-bonnet. Her husband wore a Mackintosh, which reached to his heels, and on his head an old hat, and oh, what a hat! Altogether, they were the most forlorn-looking couple one would wish to see. They carried penury in their very countenances. I pitied her so, I gave her a gentleman's dressing-gown, which had been left at the hotel. It was rather soiled, to be sure.; but then it was better than anything which she had. When she went away, she wore it off. They had started home to England, by the way of New York. When the bar-keeper requested him to register his name, he made a cross; and she was as ignorant as he. At night she asked me if I would give her a room with good fastenings to the doors and windows, as they had a good deal of gold dust with them. I inquired to know where it was, as they brought no baggage with them, except a little bag, which she carried on her arm. She said it was in belts around their waists. I told her, if it were much, she had better deliver it up to the proprietor of the house for safe keeping. Said she, "Oh, no, I would not lose sight of it for anything! I have five thousand dollars in my belt, and my husband has the same." I advised her to send it by express to New York, as they might be robbed on the way. She said they could not afford to pay the percentage for its transportation, when they could carry it, and save that money. So they started for New York by the way of Nicaragua.

I often thought of them after they left, and felt assured in my own mind that they would lose their money before they arrived home. They were two very simple people, and betrayed by their looks evident signs of fear of robbery. The next news I heard of them was, that they were both drowned at Virgin Bay, while going from the shore in a boat to get on board the steamer. The particulars were these: The boat was loaded with passengers; and, it being rather rough, they became frightened, and all rushed to one side, and capsized her. This old couple, having so much gold about their persons, sank immediately; while those who were not burdened with gold were quickly picked up by other boats. Thus these two old people, who had lived in poverty all their days, died rich, clutching the treasures for which they had toiled so hard, and to obtain which, they had denied themselves the comforts of life. The school of poverty in which they had passed the greater part of their lives, had fostered the spirit of covetousness to such a degree, that it was finally the means of their losing their lives.

CHAPTER XXI.

While in California, I had charge, for a while, of a little girl, whose mother had died just as the steamer upon which she was on board neared the wharf at San Francisco. The father, mother, and two children were on board the ill-fated Independence, which was wrecked, and then burnt, on the coast of Old California.

When she commenced burning, the father hoped to save his family from the flames by swimming with them to the shore. Being an expert swimmer, he thought that, by taking one at a time, he might succeed in bringing them all to the land. He suspended his wife over the ship's side farthest from the flames, wrapped the babe of ten months in a shawl, and consigned it to the care of a passenger until his return, took the little girl of four years in his arms, lowered himself into the water, and commenced swimming for the shore. He clasped her little arms about his neck, told her to hold on, shut her eyes and mouth, and she would soon be on the land, and then he would return for mother and the baby.

Long before they reached the land, she was senseless. In the meantime, the flames were increasing with such rapidity that it behooved the father to hasten back, in order to save his wife from the devouring element. He left the little girl senseless upon the beach, dove into the foaming surf, and was several times borne back to the shore before he could get beyond it. As he neared the burning wreck, the flames burst out afresh, forcing the frightened passengers to leap into the angry waters. The gentleman who held the babe threw it into the ocean to save himself. In its descent, the shawl became detached from it, and the child fell into the water a short distance from the mother, but beyond her reach. In one of its little hands it held a toy; and, as it was borne off on the top of a receding wave, its little plump arms were raised, and the mother saw the white, dimpled hand firmly grasping the toy. She could look no longer. Her babe was hastening on to swell the angel-band in the courts of the blessed!

When her husband reached her, the flames were close around; her dress had even been scorched. With her he started back to the shore. But very few could have breasted the angry waters as he did; but he was impelled by a motive which seemed to lend strength to his well-nigh exhausted frame. He reached the shore with his wife. Some one had found the little girl senseless, and had succeeded in restoring her to consciousness. The body of the infant was afterwards washed ashore, with the toy grasped in its hand. They made its little grave on the lonely beach, and placed it therein.

For three or four days these shipwrecked passengers remained upon the beach, their only nourishment being molasses and vinegar. They were then taken on board a vessel, and carried to San Francisco.

The mother, weakened by exposure, and suffering from a hurt which she received in her side while being suspended from the ship, breathed her last just as she was nearing their destined port.

Little Rosa (her name was Rosa Taylor) often told me the sad story in her artless, baby way. How impressive was her manner, when, seated in a little chair by my side, her dimpled face upturned, her large, dark, mournful eyes raised to mine, her rosy lips parted, to tell of the dreadful shipwreck; of the baby brother being drowned; of her being so hungry and cold on the beach; of her dear mother dying, and clasping her so closely in her arms, when she said, "Be a good girl, Rosa, and love your father; for he is all the one left to love you." Then the dying mother said, "Raise me up, and let me look upon the land once more." Then she lay back, and died.

Rosa staid with me three months, while her father was at the mines. Then he came, and took her away to Oregon.

I must not forget to mention the delights of stage-coaching in California. In the first place, the coaches are built of the strongest materials to be obtained, and are sufficiently large to carry from twenty to thirty persons. They are drawn by six large, beautiful horses. In the dry season, when the rivers are low, large boats do not run to Marysville, and most of the travel is effected by stages. I once rode to Sacramento and back in one of those six-horse coaches, when the passengers, inside and out, numbered twenty-eight. The thermometer stood at 110 deg., and the dust was so dense as to almost suffocate one. We were all obliged to *unpack* ourselves, and walk over all the bridges on the way; and then, so frail were these structures, that they trembled and swayed as the empty coach was being drawn over.

By the time you arrive at the end of your journey, your eyes, nose, and mouth are filled with dust, as well as your clothes. One day's ride ruins the clothes; but, if a person is blessed with a strong constitution, he may possibly survive several consecutive days' riding in those crowded coaches. The roads between Marysville and Sacramento are very level, it being a vast plain the whole way.

Journeying through the mountainous sections of the country in coaches, is perfectly awful. The passengers are obliged to alight, and push behind the vehicle, to assist the horses up every hill, and, when they arrive at the summit, chain the wheels, all get in, and ride to the base of the next mountain, in danger every moment of being overturned, and having their necks broken. For thus working their passages they have to pay exorbitant fares.

One night, about eleven o'clock, a lady came into the hotel, looking more dead than alive. She was leading a little girl, of about seven years of age, who was in the same plight as the mother. They were both covered with bruises, scratches, and blood, with their garments soiled and torn. They were coming from Bidwell's Bar, a place about forty miles above Marysville, in a stage-coach, in which were nine Chinamen. The coach was all closed, as it was rather cool in the mountains in the evening. All at once, they found themselves turning somersets. The coach was overturned down a steep bank.

All the Chinamen, with their long cues reaching to their heels, were rolling and tumbling about in the most ungraceful manner imaginable. They were vociferating at the top of their voices in a language which, if spoken calmly, and with the greatest mellifluence, is harsh and disagreeable in the extreme. "And," said she, "such a horrid din of voices as rang in my ears, it was scarcely possible to conceive of; which, together with the fright, was almost sufficient to deprive me of reason." The driver was seriously hurt, and so were some of the horses; but the inside passengers escaped without having any limbs broken, but their cues were awfully disarranged.

In the dry season, there were as many as a dozen coaches which left Marysville every morning, and as many would arrive every evening. Generally, they were all loaded to their utmost capacity.

In California, two-thirds of the population seem to be constantly travelling (in search of new and rich diggins, I suppose). It was quite amusing to listen to the rigmarole which each driver had over, as they reined in their horses in front of the different hotels. The names of the different localities along their routes, which they would sometimes work into laughable doggerel, the cracking of their whips, and the jokes cracked upon one another, were quite diverting.

At the time I was in Marysville, it was not safe to walk around in the suburbs of the town, in a dark evening, unless armed. Late one evening, as myself and husband were riding into town, we distinctly heard the click of a revolver, and two reports followed in quick succession. The balls whizzed past our ears, giving us no very agreeable sensation, I assure you. There was no moon, but it was starlight. Whether we were taken for people for whom some one was lying in wait, with the view of plunder or murder, or for what those shots were fired, ever remained a mystery to us. At any rate, it gave us such a fright, I never was caught out there again after dark.

There was one house in Marysville which had been in process of erection four years, and was not then completed. It was owned by a wealthy Spaniard, originally from South America. I went, one day, to view this curious structure. Under it were two regular dungeons, with heavy iron doors, which could be doubly locked and barred. People conjectured they were made for the purpose of holding his treasures, of which he was reputed to possess hoards. The whole building was the most massive, curious, complicated piece of architecture I ever beheld; and such an air of mystery and gloom as pervaded the whole place! It was impossible to elucidate the feelings one was sure to have, as they traversed those dismal-looking rooms. The sight of so much solid masonry seemed generative of the darkest designs. In one room were two very large, deep wells. Some of the floors were constructed of stone. The grounds were to be inclosed by a high wall. There were complicated wings, and high, gloomy-looking turrets, projecting in every direction from the main building. After being completed, it will present more the appearance of a prison than a private residence.

Now, I will relate one hen story; not about a renowned Shanghai, but a genuine, old-fashioned, yellow hen. Hens at that time, in California, were among the things to be coveted: the meanest specimens were sold at five dollars apiece. Some of the Spanish population kept quite a number of fowl. A lady told me she wanted to purchase a male hen; that an old Spaniard came to her house one day, who, she knew, had fowl to sell. *She* could not speak Spanish; neither could he English. She was very much perplexed how to make him know that she wanted a crower. She used every Spanish word she could think of with no success at all. Finally, she sprang up in a chair, flapped her arms, and crowed with all her might. That crow enlightened the Spaniard more than all her Spanish vocabulary had done.

When I lived in the canvas shanty, a partition of cloth ran across the centre of the building. On one side of the partition stood my bed, and on the other my brother's. An outer door opened into this room. One day, an old yellow hen walked in very unceremoniously, hopped upon the bed, and prepared to lay. Soon she jumped off, and left an egg. She conducted the whole affair with the greatest secrecy, not even indulging in that greatest luxury of all, cackling. Of course, I fed her, very glad indeed of her egg, as they were fifty cents apiece. The next day, she came again, and left another; and so she kept on, until she had laid twelve; when she evinced symptoms of a desire to sit upon the nest. My brother took her eggs, carried them out to a ranch, and exchanged them for those that would be sure to hatch. He then placed them in a half barrel in the corner of the room, and set the hen upon them. In due time she brought out twelve little chicks. When they were about a month old, I sold them for a dollar apiece. She then laid another litter of eggs, and was as successful in raising another brood of chickens. Then, as we were going to leave the shanty, I sold her, chickens and all, for twenty dollars.

After I had been living at the Tremont some time, I went to my room one day, and there, on the window-seat, was perched the identical old hen that I had sold. My window was open, and she had flown in. She appeared delighted to see me, and evinced her delight by singing quite merrily. She seemed determined to room with me, and I allowed her to remain until I could go and find the one to whom I sold her. He had moved, and was not to be found. Of course, the hen was mine again; but, situated as I now was, I could not accommodate her with a room in the house, and for which she seemed to have a decided predilection. I therefore placed her to board out on a ranch. She continued to lay eggs and raise chickens, until I realized, from the sale of them, forty-five dollars. I then sold her again for five dollars, as she was getting rather old. In one week after I sold her, she died, from *grief, I suppose, at being sold.* From that old yellow hen I made quite a *pile,* as they say in California.

CHAPTER XXII.

I RECOLLECT the execution of one man in Marysville, which created quite an excitement in town. One day my ears were assailed with the most piercing shrieks. Upon inquiry, I learned that a man had been arrested by the Vigilance Committee for stealing. A great crowd had collected in the street in front of the committee's rooms, among whom was the wife of the man arrested; and hers were the shrieks which rent the air. Two little children were following her, crying, "You shall not hang my father! you must not kill him!" Finally the committee rendered him up into the hands of the law. He had his trial, was condemned, and sentenced to be hung. While he was in jail, awaiting his execution, a lady in town gave a little party for her children. While they were taking tea, she saw the two children of the doomed man going past. Pity for the children, so soon to be left fatherless, incited her to call them in, and seat them at the table spread with delicacies. After they had partaken of the treat, and gone out to play, the girl who was clearing the table missed one of the silver spoons. Something prompted her to go to those two children to inquire for it. She thought the boy betrayed signs of guilt. She took hold of his arm, and felt the spoon in his jacket-sleeve. He cried bitterly, and said he did not want to steal, but his mother told him if he did not, whenever he had an opportunity, she would whip him severely. Perhaps the father had been stimulated to commit thefts by similar threats from his wife; and certainly, if her evil propensities had so far gained the ascendency as to cause her to instil such principles into the minds of her children, to what evils would she not resort, to gain her object?

The night previous to the day upon which he was to be executed, she made an attempt to fire the city, in the hope, doubtless, that her accomplices in guilt would effect his liberation while the

20*

attention of the citizens would be directed to the fire. She was, however, unsuccessful. Had the stable burnt which she attempted to fire, the whole city would probably have been destroyed. The owner of the stable had just returned from a journey, and was throwing some hay into the rack for his horse. In the meantime, she approached, ignited a bunch of matches, and thrust them under the side of the building, directly against this hay-rack. It blazed up, which the man no sooner saw than he caught a large blanket, threw it into the rack, and jumped down upon it. By this means, the flames were extinguished, but not, however, without quite severely scorching the man. She was carefully guarded after this.

The next day, she begged permission to visit her husband in his cell. She was allowed to go, but not alone; but, somehow or other, she managed (they supposed) to slip something into his hand, for, a short time after the interview, when they went to take him to the gallows, they found him insensible, whether from fear, or from something which he had taken, they could not ascertain.

He was taken to the gallows, and the forms of execution enacted, although he manifested no appearance of life whatever. While this last act was being performed, it required six or seven women to hold the wife. She was perfectly frantic.

Every day, for some time after, might be seen this woman, dressed in a garb of the deepest mourning, holding each of her children by the hand, and traversing the streets, apparently in great distress. It was thought she made this public display of grief to excite sympathy. Soon after this, she disappeared from the city.

It often made me feel sad, during my residence in California, to see the people recently from the Atlantic states so hopeful and buoyant in spirits, anticipating such rich harvests of gold, with which they would return to their homes and families, I knew so well the sufferings and hardships they would be likely to endure before they could return, if they ever did. But I ever refrained from casting a shade of melancholy over the bright future in prospective by prophetic warnings. I recollect one gentleman in particular, who was *so* sanguine of success.

He departed for the mines, and, in three months from that time, was brought back, crippled for life! While blasting rocks, he had one arm so shattered that he was obliged to have it amputated above the elbow. Both eyes were rendered sightless for life, and the other hand and arm very much injured. What a pitiable-looking object he was! and how he begged of the doctors to use every endeavor to save the remaining hand and arm! He had a wife and three little children in the state of Maine, dependent on him for a support. It was in vain the doctors tried, by extracting piece after piece of splintered rock, to save the last hand. It was amputated at the wrist. How philosophically he bore his sufferings! Not a groan escaped his lips; but, by the workings of his countenance, one could perceive his agony was extreme. Money was raised in Marysville sufficient to defray his expenses home; and a fellow-townsman of the sufferer volunteered to accompany him as nurse. I never heard aught concerning him again.

I often amused myself for hours, studying, not human nature, but mule nature. It is really astonishing to witness those pack-mules, and see the wonderful knowledge they display by their manoeuvres. In packing them for a trip to the mountains, the Mexicans load them unmercifully. They make them carry loads weighing from three hundred to three hundred and fifty pounds, and strap the articles on so tightly that I should think it would stop their breaths. The poor creatures will tremble under such an unmerciful load, and sometimes I have seen them, after going a little way, fall from exhaustion, and the weight of their load. Then those cruel Mexicans would beat them, until the blood would run from their noses; and, if they were very much reduced from previous hard usage, they would die, with that heavy pack strapped to them. These pack-mules have such a horror of going with their loads to the mountains, that, after they are packed, and are waiting for the remainder of the train, (these trains sometimes consist of fifty and sixty mules,) they will endeavor to secrete themselves away behind some building or wagon, and keep so very still and quiet, seemingly listening and hoping they may not be found. By and by, when the old, cruel Mexican warns them of his presence by a heavy slap with the piece of untanned hide he invariably carries in his hand, accompanied with the expression of *hippa, mula!* one can almost see a shade of the deepest despair cross the poor mule's countenance, as he joins the train, which is going to travel many weary, tedious miles, over rough mountains, and through deep ravines.

These trains are led by a horse, with a bell attached to his neck. He is designated the bell-horse; and these mules have such an affection for him, that they will follow anywhere he goes. Generally, three or four Mexicans accompany each train. When night overtakes them, they unpack the animals, and form a sort of corral of the pack-saddles, which they place in a circle around the goods, which they lay in piles, each load beside the saddle upon which it belongs. The mules are turned out to graze. In the morning, after giving them their breakfasts, at a signal from the Mexicans, each mule places himself in a position to be packed beside his own saddle; and, what is very singular, each mule knows his own saddle, and never makes a mistake by placing himself beside his neighbor's.

When they return to the valley again, they are so delighted, that when they get to within a mile or two of the town, they commence running, and braying at the top of their voices. And then look out for the dust! Such clouds of it as they will raise in passing a house, is almost suffocating. You must hasten, and close the doors and windows, otherwise the house will be filled.

"As stubborn as a mule," is an old adage; and I have seen this maxim verified oftentimes. I have seen them so obstinate, you might kill, but never conquer. Perhaps it is this stubborn nature which some of them (not all) possess, that causes the Mexicans to be so ugly to them. In order to pack some of them, they are obliged to be chained and blinded. What struggles I have seen between the Mexican and his mule! I have heard them say, that a real malicious one would purposely run, so that he could dash with great violence his pack against a rock or tree, and smash it to pieces; then, if it contained ought eatable, devour it with all haste before the driver could reach him. And many such "ugly capers" are imputed to his muleship.

At one time, there was great excitement in the mountains respecting the mysterious disappearance of a man named Dunbar, who kept a public-house on the trail leading from Marysville to Onion Valley, on Slate Creek. These public-houses, by the way, were nothing more than little shanties; and the only servant generally employed about them was a cook. Travellers who passed and repassed Dunbar's house, and found no one there but his cook, (a young man formerly from Lowell, Massachusetts,) naturally inquired for Dunbar, and was told that he had gone to San Francisco. Finally, the house was closed. Then suspicions were rife that there had been foul play. About that time, as a hunter was passing the deserted house, his dog ran into the corral, and began scratching in the snow, and howling incessantly. His master in vain tried to call him away. He then went to the spot, dug away the snow, and discovered a man's hand and arm protruding from the earth. He dug away the earth, and there was the body of Dunbar, bent double, thus tied with a rope, and stamped into that slight excavation.

The cook, very naturally, was the first person suspected of perpetrating this horrid murder. He was traced to San Francisco and arrested, just as he was stepping on board a steamer bound to Panama. He was accused of the murder, appeared very much agitated, and finally confessed what he knew about the affair. One night, two people came from a mining locality near by to Dunbar's house, and requested a night's lodging. They frequently came there, and passed the night. That evening, they played cards with Dunbar; and, in the course of the evening, he had occasion to go to a chest which stood in the room, and deposit some money. In this chest was about five thousand dollars. Whether they saw it, or whether he told them he had it, he (the cook) did not know.

One of the men came to him in the kitchen, and disclosed their intentions of murdering Dunbar that night, and securing his money, which they would share with him, if he would take an oath of eternal secrecy; if not, his life would pay the forfeit. Fear compelled him to agree to this proposal. Just then, Dunbar and the other villain came into the kitchen, and advanced to the outer door; whereupon the other one caught up an axe near by, and struck Dunbar a blow on the back of the head, causing him to fall. Then followed another blow, which completed the work of death. He was then buried as above described, and the money taken possession of by the murderers. Said he, "They offered me a share of their ill-gotten treasures; but no — I would not pollute my fingers by receiving one dollar of their blood-stained gold. Dunbar was a friend to me, and gladly would I have saved him from the horrid death which awaited him, had it been in my power so to do; but I was paralyzed with terror at the horrid revelation to which I had just listened. When they departed, I should have hastened to some authority, and made instant disclosure of the whole transaction; but was deterred from so doing by the fear of being murdered by those fiends in human shape.

"I then determined to leave the country; which determination I was in the act of putting into execution when arrested.

"I declare to you, I am innocent of all or any participation whatever in the horrid affair."

The two murderers were at once arrested. They had changed their place of residence, but were soon ferreted out; and all three were sentenced to be hung at Slate Creek. My brother was present at the execution. The two murderers died as they had lived — hardened sinners — profaning and blaspheming until the last.

The cook declared his innocence to the latest moment, and begged, even after the rope was adjusted about his neck, to be allowed to write to his wife. This boon was granted him. He then asked if he might make a few remarks. He commenced; and so eloquently did he plead for pardon, so heart-softening were his remarks, that, had not the mob been so exasperated by previous horrid disclosures made by the two murderers, he would and ought to have been pardoned. They had gone so far as to say, "All who are in favor of hanging this man, go down the hill; and all who are not, go up;" and, as the majority started to go down the hill, some of the more ferocious ones caught the rope, and ran with it, jerking him from the ground, and consummating a murder equally as cold-blooded as the one for which that innocent man had been arraigned.

One more story of blood and murder I will relate, and then close the calendar of murders. As I was sitting in the parlor, one day, I saw the people in the street all running towards the front of the hotel. I stepped out upon the balcony to ascertain the cause of this unusual excitement, and beheld a sight that almost curdled the blood in my veins. There lay the form of a man, dead. His clothes were saturated with blood; his ghastly face upturned; and upon his death-stamped features rested a look of mortal agony. It was the body of one well known in our midst. He was coming from one of the mining bars above Marysville, driving a mule-team, when he was accosted by a man whom he overtook on the road with a request to give him a ride; which request he accordingly granted. The stranger jumped into the wagon, and took a seat behind the teamster. They conversed as they rode along, until they came to an unfrequented part of the road, when the stranger suddenly plunged a knife into the body of the teamster. It was a murderous blow, and carried death in its unerring aim. He robbed the dying man of four hundred dollars, which he had in his pocket, and then decamped. The man was not instantly killed, but, before he breathed his last, was found by a traveller, to whom he told the story, and also gave a description of the murderer, who was afterwards taken and executed. The murdered man left a wife and family to mourn his loss.

Many more murders, equally revolting, I might recount; but I have told enough to give one an idea of the crime existing at that time in California. I need not say, at that time; it still exists, and, I fear, ever will. Vigilance committees may, for a while, intimidate the blood-thirsty villains; but they can never rid the country of *all* those pests of society who have there congregated to feast their evil propensities upon the lives and property of the unwary and unsuspecting.

Early in the year 1849, an enterprising, energetic young man, left the town of D——, situated in one of the Western States, to seek his fortune in California. He was already in possession of a sum sufficient to defray his expenses to those golden shores, which held forth so many charms to an adventurous spirit, leaving but little remaining in his purse upon his arrival.

Glittering visions of lumps of gold haunted his waking, as well as sleeping, moments. He was restless and impatient, until he found himself bounding gayly over the wild, heaving billows of the broad Atlantic. Being an orphan, deprived, at an early age, of the watchful tenderness of a mother's love, the judicious precepts and examples of a father, he had learned early in life the salutary lesson of self-reliance. No sad yearnings filled his heart, as he paced the steamer's deck on the eve of departure. The delights and social joys of a pleasant home left behind, the remembrance of a loving mother's tearful farewell, rose not in his mind, to cause the tear of affection and regret to bedew his cheek. He was leaving none behind to mourn his departure. To him the future looked bright and beautiful, as it ever does to the young, hopeful, and aspiring heart, over which the chilling waves and bitter disappointments of the cold, selfish world has never rolled.

There was one passenger on board, who, from his taciturn, repulsive manner, had made no friends, and formed no acquaintances. A few days before their arrival at Chagres, he was missed from his accustomed seat at table. He no more paced the deck with that quick, uncertain tread, ever accompanied with those nervous, stealthy glances bestowed on all around, and which had occasioned so many remarks at his expense, by no means flattering or complimentary. He was confined to his berth from sickness.

They reached the isthmus of Panama. All were hastening to secure their passage upon the steamer then waiting at Panama to convey them to their destined port. Each and all were struggling for themselves. The party to which the hero of my story had attached himself were toiling on their "winding way," when their attention was attracted to a hammock, suspended between two trees, in which, to all appearance, lay a man in the agonies of death. They hastened to his side, and discovered, to their surprise, the repulsive stranger of steamer memory. In a feeble voice, he besought them, in mercy, to take him along, and not leave him to die alone! It appeared he had employed some natives to take him across the isthmus. They had quarrelled among themselves, purloined the last dollar from the sick man, (Mr. B——,) and vamosed, leaving him to the fatē which was inevitable, unless he was assisted and provided for immediately. The hot fever-blood was coursing wildly through his swollen veins; yet there was but one, in that company of men, whose heart was touched by the appealing looks of the apparently dying man, or whose eye moistened as the half-articulate words were gasped, "Oh! in God's name, leave me not here, to die alone!"

As some extenuation for the apparently heartless course pursued by all that company of emigrants, (all except one,) I will state their relative circumstances. They had purchased their tickets at an exorbitant price, with perhaps the last dollar at their command. The steamer was waiting; time was pressing; at such a day she was going to leave Panama, and, if not there, they lost their passage. Panama was crowded with people, waiting to get even a foothold upon the deck of any floating craft that would bear them to the desired haven. The delay that must necessarily accrue from assisting that suffering person would, in all probability, cost them their passage, and they would be left penniless in a foreign land.

The call of suffering humanity was counterbalanced by the whisperings of self. They soliloquized, and hushed the breathings of conscience with thoughts like these: "I must look to my own interest. No one would lend a helping hand to raise *me*, if I were sinking. He did not make friends with us when in health and prosperity; but now, when he is dying, he calls for succor from those he formerly shunned. I cannot assist him. He will probably die before night. I must hurry on." So they did hurry on, all except Mr. W——. *His* heart was boiling over with the "milk of human kindness." Said he, "If I go on, and leave this man to die alone, the image of his pale, sad face will be ever by my side. The memory of my heartless conduct will cast a dark shade over my whole future existence. I *cannot* and I *will not* be so soulless."

In a softened voice he addressed the now nearly unconscious man, and, taking the feverish hand in his, said he, "Cease your anxiety. I will stay with you, and take care of you." One by one, he saw all his company depart; and he was alone with the sick one, in the unbroken solitudes of a Granadian forest. He held a flask of water to the lips of the sufferer, and bathed his fevered brow. This somewhat revived him. Hours passed on, and they were still alone. Finally, two Carthaginians came along, and were induced, by the promise of a liberal reward, to carry the sick man to Panama. After a toilsome journey, which well-nigh proved fatal to Mr. B——, they arrived at Panama, but were too late for the steamer: she had been gone nearly a day. There was no alternative but to wait until they could secure a passage upon another. Mr. W——'s funds were fast dwindling away before the exorbitant demands of the Panama "land-sharks." Who, among those who were compelled to remain there days and weeks, when the tide of emigration was rushing irresistibly on towards the far-famed gold placers of California, can *ever* forget the merciless drain upon their purses?

When able to converse, the invalid informed Mr. W—— that he had a valuable cargo on board a vessel then on her way around Cape Horn; and that, upon her arrival at San Francisco, in part payment of the debt of gratitude he owed to him, he (Mr. W——) should receive a share of the profits derived from the sale thereof. He also spoke of a failure in business which had occurred a short time previous to his departure; but omitted to mention, however, the fact that he had acted very dishonestly as regarded that failure, and also that he had been very unceremoniously smuggled on board the steamer, to elude the vigilance of officers of justice. He expected his wife to join him soon in California: perhaps she might come on the next steamer.

They were detained in Panama four weeks, during which time he was carefully nursed by Mr. W——. In the meantime, his wife arrived, with money sufficient to purchase a ticket for her husband. Mr. W—— had not the wherewithal to purchase one; therefore, he procured a situation as waiter on board. Upon their arrival at San Francisco, as the ship was not due for some two months, Mr. W—— concluded to proceed at once to the mines.

Every day, at that time, might have been seen little companies of men, with their blankets and tin pans strapped to their backs, commencing their toilsome march into the interior. Far up those mighty streams they wandered, and penetrated far into the solitary fastnesses of those mountain gorges, where the foot of white man never trod before. Forming one of a party of miners who followed the course of the American River, was our friend W——. For three weary months they prospected in those dreary wilds, camping out, rolling themselves in their blankets, with no roof to shelter them from the night air. The twinkling stars, far, far above them, peeping out a gentle good-night from the azure dome, were like messengers of hope to those poor wayfarers. Sickness overtook them, and death·

thinned their numbers. Out of a company of ten, but three returned to San Francisco. One of those three was Mr. W——. Sick, disheartened, and so emaciated he could scarcely support his feeble frame, he dragged himself to the door of the only hospital in San Francisco, and begged for admittance.

For many weeks he lay hovering at the portal of death's mysterious door. Finally, a strong constitution triumphed: this once, the destroying angel was cheated of its prey. He recovered slowly, and, at the expiration of many weeks, found himself treading the streets of San Francisco, weak, penniless, and alone — alone, in a land of strangers. He bethought himself of Mr. B——, made inquiries concerning him, and ascertained that the ship had arrived which had contained his property; that he had disposed of it at an immense profit, and had gone to reside in Sacramento city. Slowly and painfully he dragged his weakened frame to one of the piers from whence departed the up-river boats, and gained a hearing with one of the captains, to whom he stated his situation. He very kindly gave him a passage to "Sac' city." When landed upon the Levee, it was mid-day. So weak was he, that it was late in the afternoon before he reached the residence of Mr. B——. Upon inquiring for that gentleman, Mrs. B—— made her appearance. She did not recognize him at first, so changed was he by sickness and poverty. Then, in cold, heartless words, she expressed her sorrow at his unfortunate condition, hoped he would get along without any more sickness, and coolly closed the door in his face.

Imagine his feelings as he turned from that door, sick in body, and sicker far at heart at this display of sordid selfishness and heartless ingratitude. He crawled back again to the Levee, where he remained that night, supperless, shelterless, and penniless. He again solicited a passage to Marysville, where resided an acquaintance of his who kept a hotel. To him he applied for a situation to work; for, sick as he was, his independent spirit spurned the idea of begging. He was at once engaged to wash dishes; for which service he received seventy-five dollars per month. After serving awhile in this capacity, he was promoted to steward, with an increase of salary. From this post he was admitted as a partner; and, from that day, "Dame Fortune" lavished upon him her richest gifts.

Just three years from the time he composed his wearied limbs for a night's rest, in the open air, on the banks of the Sacramento, he was standing again upon the same spot, but under what different auspices! Had prosperity changed his noble heart, that, a little more than three years ago, listened and "wept for others' woes"? Ah, no! the same generous impulses governed his every action. His upright, honest principles grew and strengthened with his fortune, instead of deteriorating, as is oftentimes the case.

Curiosity prompted him to inquire after the welfare of Mr. B——. He learned he was a houseless vagabond around the streets of San Francisco. From affluence, he was reduced to a state of beggary. His wife had proved faithless, and decamped with all the money she could get. In endeavoring to drown his sorrow in the intoxicating cup, he had lost, dollar by dollar, the remainder of his fortune. That for which he had sacrificed honor, principle, and every trait which ennobles and exalts man, had "taken to itself wings," and the misguided man was bereft of all which renders life a blessing. From this "ower true" tale may be deduced a moral.

CHAPTER XXIII.

In the fall of 1852, my brother was in the mines, on the north fork of the Yuba, about one hundred miles above Marysville. As the rainy season was commencing, and knowing his claims to be on the river, where they could not be worked except in the dry season, I was daily expecting him to arrive in Marysville, as he had written to that effect; yet he came not. Daily I heard accounts of large quantities of snow falling; and it finally fell to such a depth, that all communication with the settlements in the mountains was cut off before the winter's supply of provisions had been transported thither. Fears were entertained that the mountain population would suffer incredibly for the want of food; and so they did. Finally, a straggling, emaciated, exhausted party arrived in town from Downieville, which is eighty miles distant from Marysville.

Fifty miles of the route they had traversed over snow, which lay to the depth of ten and fifteen feet, and part of the time sinking, at every step, up to their arm-pits in it. Two or three of their number had given out and died on the way. The reports they brought were dismal in the extreme. They said the entire male population would be obliged to leave Downieville, and get to Marysville, if possible, or die in the attempt, as there were only provisions enough in town when they left to supply the women and children.

What anxiety I felt on my brother's account, knowing that he must depend upon Downieville for his supplies! No tidings whatever could I obtain of him, and did not for four months. During this time, remnants of parties were arriving, completely exhausted, and reporting great distress in the mountains. At the expiration of that time, the express-men opened for themselves a passage through the snow. Then I received a letter, stating the following particulars:

He had made every preparation for leaving his log cabin as soon as there was any appearance of snow, when one of his partners (he had two) was violently seized with the mountain fever. Then came the first fall of snow. What could they do? They could not leave him to die alone, and it was impossible to move him. For one month he was constantly delirious. He had no physician to attend him, and there he lay, day and night, talking to his mother and friends at home, in happy unconsciousness of his deplorable situation. The snow fell until it lay to the depth of fifteen feet.

Downieville was twenty miles distant, and thither one of them must go to obtain provisions; for they were entirely destitute of everything in the eatable line, and almost destitute of money. They had sent their gold to Marysville the day before the partner was taken sick, reserving only sufficient to defray their expenses down.

My brother started to go to Downieville, previously assisting his partner to tie the sick man on to his pallet of straw; for, in moments of violent delirium, one person could not compete with him in strength.

In an exhausted state he reached Downieville, and found provisions very scarce, and dear as gold dust. For ham he paid eighty cents per pound; for flour, one dollar and a half per pound; and everything in a like proportion. For one ten pounds of flour, which he bought during the winter, he paid twenty-five dollars. He wanted to get some corn meal to make gruel for the sick man, and succeeded in getting one pound, for which he paid the exorbitant sum of two dollars.

With a back-load of provisions — which weighed sixty-one pounds, and cost one hundred dollars — he started back. Several times, on the way, he felt as if he should never live to reach the little cabin; but he finally arrived there. "Oh," said he, "what dreary days and nights we passed in that log cabin, listening to the moanings of the sick man, whom we were hourly expecting to breathe his last, surrounded and hemmed in by impassable barriers of snow! We could not wile away the time evenings by reading, for we had no oil or candles: a little grease in a tin plate, with a rag in it, was all we had to light in case of emergency. Our cabin was completely covered with snow. We kept a hole open from the door up to the surface. Mornings, upon going out, the foot-prints of large grisly bears would be all around in the snow, over the top of the cabin. When we had consumed all the provisions which I had taken up, we both started again for more, leaving the sick man alone; but he was wholly unconscious, and never knew of our absence. What little we could get this time was even higher than before; and the climate had a tendency to give us such good appetites. We boiled those ham bones until they were as white as polished ivory. For two or three days we subsisted upon water-gruel.

"I then started again for Downieville, so hungry

and faint, I thought I should never reach there. I had no money; but a trader in Downieville, who was acquainted with my circumstances, kindly offered to furnish me with provisions, upon credit. As I was passing a hotel, I smelled the dinner, and stepped upon the stoop, wishing — oh, how earnestly! — that I had the wherewithal to procure a dinner. But I was 'flat broke,' as the saying is there, when one is out of funds. Presently I was accosted by a fellow who once mined with me in the country. Said he, 'What is the matter, Bryant? What makes you look so down-hearted? Are you flat broke?' — 'Yes,' said I, 'and starving, besides.' — 'Not while I have the color,' said he, and put five dollars into my hand. With this I bought myself a good dinner; and it was a wonder I survived it, for I assure you I did eat some.

"Thus we lived on for four long, weary months. The fever settled in the sick man's toes, and they all decayed. Finally, he began to convalesce; but it was six months from the time he was taken with the fever before he was able to walk. How grateful he felt to us, who had almost sacrificed our lives to stay by and nurse him! He would cry, and say, 'If I am ever worth a fortune, you shall share it with me.' Before I left the country, he had been able to earn a little money. He came to see me, and proffered the whole, as he said, to compensate, in a measure, for my kindness to him. Of course, I refused to accept of one dollar; for he then looked too feeble to work.

"During all these winter months, we never shot but one deer; and then we feasted! The snow lay to such a depth, we could not go hunting; and game was very scarce, too.

"The provisions which we consumed during three months amounted to five hundred dollars, and then never had as much as would satisfy our appetites at any one meal."

My brother described the snow-slides in the mountains as grand and frightful. A body of snow would commence rolling at the summit of a mountain, collecting and increasing in size as it rolled, until it came with such velocity, and in such a mass, that it would snap off large trees in its descent as easily as if they had been whip-sticks. One could hear the rushing, roaring sound it made, for miles. It is necessary to build their cabins in such a position that they will not be in danger of annihilation from these slides. Cabins have been swept away, and the inmates killed, by snow-slides.

As soon as the rocks around the cabin began to

get bare, they began to crevice for gold. One night, while his partner was preparing supper, my brother took out seventeen dollars (in little lumps) with a crevicing-spoon.

A lady once told me, who had lived in the mountains, that every day, after her housework was done up, she would take her crevicing-spoon, and go out among the rocks searching for gold. She resided there one year, and, during that time, had collected five hundred dollars in that way.

When the spring opened, my brother concluded to remain through the dry season, and for eighteen months he was a dweller in those mountain solitudes, and not once during that time visiting the valley. In his rambles, one day, he found the skeleton of a human being. What sad reflections the sight of those bones called up! He dug a grave, and buried them.

The grisly bears were quite plenty around them; and one day, while they were out mining, "Old Bruin" made a descent into their cabin, helping himself to everything the place contained, and overturning tin pans, pots, and kettles, and everything within his reach. He swallowed all their butter, for which they had paid one dollar and a half per pound, and marched off, no doubt delighted with the feast he had enjoyed at the expense of the poor miners. When they returned, tired and hungry, to their shanty, to prepare their frugal meal, they were struck with the utmost consternation at beholding the havoc made within, — by whom, they readily conjectured, for there were his large footprints, very conspicuous. Then there was no alternative but to go, tired as they were, to Downieville, (twenty miles,) and back up more provisions. Then they baited old Bruin with a piece of meat, loaded their guns, and lay in wait for him all day and night; but he never came again. Whether his digestive organs were incapable of performing the necessary functions after such an expensive feast; or whether he was so cunning as to suspect they would watch for his return, they never knew.

At one time an old hunter came to their cabin with his dog, and reported himself to be very expert at killing grislys. They took their guns, and accompanied him. They soon routed an enormously large bear, whose roar seemed to shake the earth. He first turned his attention to the dog, which appeared terribly frightened, and ran away as fast as his legs would carry him. Then he turned upon the brave hunters, who quickly followed the example of the dog. They fled to some tall trees, upon which there was not a limb for twenty or thirty feet from the base. They exerted every faculty to shin up those naked trunks. My brother, who was not a little frightened, thought that, at least, he was twenty feet from the ground, when, upon looking down, he found he was not more than five. How he redoubled his efforts! for the bear was making after them at a furious rate. After clearing the field of his antagonists, and giving two or three tremendous roars in honor of victory, he marched off into the surrounding forest. After this, they were engaged in several more successful bear-hunts.

At one time, he was mining on Cañon Creek, and had occasion to cross the mountains to Slate Range. Many of these mountains are perennially covered with snow. When travelling in the mountains, clothes more than you have on your back are burdensome and unnecessary.

After going a short distance from the camp, he hung an overcoat on the limb of a tree, set his carpet-bag at the foot of it, and buried what gold he had with him at a short distance from the tree, carefully noting the spot. He then pursued his journey. Upon arriving at his destination, his mining operations detained him there eight months.

When he returned, he found his coat hanging upon the same limb; his carpet-bag was unmolested; and he found his gold just as he had left it. Clothes, in the mountains, are no temptation to a person's cupidity, if he has a suit on his back.

At one time, in company with two or three others, started to go from one mining locality to another. They were obliged to camp out for four nights upon the snow; and in some of the deep ravines, which were filled by the sliding of the snow into them, they judged it to be at least fifty feet in depth. Nights, they would roll themselves in their blankets, and lie down upon the snow, with nought above them but the blue dome of the star-lighted heavens, and sleep as soundly, and be visited by dreams as sweet, as ever blessed their midnight slumbers in nicely carpeted chambers, on beds of down.

CHAPTER XXIV.

Before I leave California, I must give you a sketch of John Chinaman, — not the Johns in general, but a particular John, who lived in the

Tremont Hotel as a chamber servant for more than a year. He could talk good broken English, was quick in his motions, and very neat. I liked John better than any other of the chamber servants, he was so faithful. Often I would be so amused at his remarks, that I would have to stop, and laugh heartily. Then he would look *so* perplexed, and say, "What you laughee so for, Missa Bessa?" He invariably called the name Bates, Bessa.

He had been in California four years, during all of which time he had been out to service, never receiving less than one hundred dollars per month. He had about three thousand dollars out at interest, for which he received three per cent. a month. He was very penurious, never indulging in any luxury, save most excellent tea, which he kept for his own private use.

Sometimes, when I would be sick, he would come to my door, bringing a cup of his tea, and say, "You drinkee this, Missa Bessa; make you well quick." He placed implicit faith in the healing properties of his tea.

His money, his tea, and his cue were his especial delight. Days when he would have a great deal to do, engaging his time until late in the evening, he would never retire, however tired he might be, without first combing, oiling, and braiding his cue. This he kept coiled around on the top of his head; and, instead of keeping the remaining portion of his pate shaved, as they generally do, he allowed it to grow, and kept it cut, after the fashion of the Americans. When he had his hat upon his head, one would never suppose he had a cue. He was the best-looking Chinaman I ever saw, and came from Ningpo.

Upon first arriving in California, he went as house servant to Senator Gwin. Afterwards, he lived with a Mr. Peck. He would say sometimes, "Only three very good ladees in Californee." — "Who are those, John?" — "Missa Gwina, Missa Pecka, and Missa Bessa. Missa Gwina, she one very good ladee; she talkee, laughee, all day long, eat watermelon, drink champagne; she one very good ladee." John seemed to estimate the qualifications of Mrs. Gwin by the quantity of good and expensive things which she ate and drank. Watermelons were twelve dollars apiece, and champagne ten dollars per bottle. Then he would say, "Missa Pecka one very good ladee, but she too fatter. Missa Bessa, she no too fatter; she too smallee, too sickee (sometimes I would have ill turns); she go home to her mudder; me go too. She too smallee; I be her servant." He seemed very much attached to me, and was always ready and willing to wait upon me.

One day, he was very unceremoniously rushed into matrimony. The particulars of this hurried marriage were as follows: John was one day passing along one of the streets occupied mostly by Chinese, when his ears were assailed with horrid screams which issued from a building near by. He burst in the door, which was fastened, and there found a Canton Chinaman unmercifully beating one of his slaves, a young girl of about sixteen years. John, who was very tender-hearted, could not bear to see that; so he knocked down the Chinaman, took the girl, whom he never saw until then, and ran with her to the hotel, and wanted me to secrete her in my room. It appears there is an almost deadly feud existing between the Canton and Ningpo Chinamen. As soon as the Canton Chinaman recovered himself sufficiently to realize what had happened, he collected about thirty of his partisans, and started to arrest John for assaulting him, and carrying off his slave.

This was apprehended by the people at the hotel, who all felt very much interested for John. They told him, in order to prevent the girl from being taken back by her cruel master, he must marry her. Then he could retain her as his wife; but could not be sustained in secreting away another's slave. To this arrangement John readily acquiesced, and was hurried off to an esquire; an interpreter obtained, — for the bride elect could not articulate one word of English, — and the ceremony commenced. When John was asked if he would take that woman to be his wedded wife, his reply was, "Yes, me takee her: me lovee her; she lovee me. Canton Chinaman no get her, no whipee her. Me be good to her; take good care of her. She be my little wife!" And he ran on with such a tirade, they thought they should never check him.

They were married before her master found her; and therefore he never recovered his slave. John had a small house in the back yard of the hotel, and in it he placed his wife. She was not domestic at all, and there she sat with her hands folded, when not engaged in embroidering. And there I left them when I started for the States.

Most of the washing and ironing in California is performed by Chinamen. They take the clothes to the rivers, and beat them on stones and boards, which they place in particular positions. Their clothes-lines are stretched all along the banks of the river. After the articles are dry, they take them to their houses to iron. They starch every article, even to sheets and pillow-slips. Their mode of ironing is entirely different from anything I ever before saw. They have a copper vessel, shaped like a sauce-pan, and large enough to hold about two quarts of coal. The bottom of this vessel is very thick, and highly polished. They fill it with burning coal; then take hold of the handle, and shove it back and forth over the articles.

They have a dish of water standing beside them, to which they put their mouths, and draw up such a quantity of the water, that their cheeks are inflated to their utmost capacity. All the while they are shoving this vessel back and forth, they are blowing the water out of their mouths, which falls like spray upon the garment, and renders it of an equal dampness. They iron very smoothly, and the clothes have a beautiful polish. For ironing dresses, they have differently shaped sauce-pans. They wear out the clothes very much beating them so; and it is almost dangerous to stand in the vicinity of their washing resorts, the shirt-buttons fly so like hail-stones.

There is a place, a little out from San Francisco,

called Washerwoman's Bay, where the Chinamen take all the clothes from the city to wash. I once took a walk out there; and, before I came in sight of the bay, I heard the noise occasioned by the clothes being thrashed so unmercifully. While I stood listening, not well assured of the cause of that peculiar noise, a gentleman appeared, coming in the direction from whence the sounds proceeded. I asked him what that noise was. Said he, "You are in close proximity to Washerwoman's Bay; and I would advise you to go no farther, if you value your life; for the shirt-buttons are flying so thick, and with such velocity, it is really dangerous to go too near."

A short time before I left Marysville, the city was visited by another conflagration, which came very near destroying the Tremont Hotel. It occurred between ten and eleven o'clock, one Sunday. The fire originated in the square directly opposite the hotel; and, what wind there was being fair to bring it directly to the house, the greatest consternation prevailed. The ladies were all dressed to attend church. They commenced packing their things, and throwing them out the doors and windows. The proprietor ordered every woollen blanket in the house to be produced, wet thoroughly, and then nailed them all over that part of the house most exposed to the flames. One part of the building had a flat roof, upon which barrels of water were kept standing, also a number of pails. This roof was covered with people, passing and throwing water to prevent ignition.

While this was going on outside, the people were rushing in, and removing beds and furniture. In their haste to remove large pieces, they tore down partitions, and otherwise injured the house; breaking out windows, sash and all, to eject some piece of furniture. Individuals who had been boarding in the house, and had not deposited their money in the safe, ran to their trunks, took it out, and gave it to me for safe keeping. I had my pockets so filled with gold and gold dust, it was really burthensome to move about. The most valuable things were removed out on the plains, and I stood guard over them; for they required strict watching, there were so many standing round, ready to take anything they could lay their hands upon. Several times the roof of the hotel was on fire; but, by the strenuous exertions of the people, it was extinguished. The flames were darting over and around it, yet the building was preserved, at the risk, almost, of their own lives. The proprietor's face was scorched quite badly, as he was ever in the van; and where the most danger was, there he was sure to be seen. The building was saved; but what a looking house to return to! Every part ran with mud and water; the partitions were demolished, and windows broken; all the blankets which belonged upon the beds, wet and dirty on the outside of the house. But they soon dried; and that night, by ten o'clock, there were beds ready to accommodate a hundred persons. How we all worked! I never recollect being so tired, before or since, as I was that night. When I left Marysville, the old hotel was standing in all its pristine beauty. It had withstood all the fires which had visited Marysville during the space of three years; but I had only been at home three months, when tidings reached me that it was burned to the ground.

CHAPTER XXV.

In the spring of 1854, I bade adieu to Marysville, and started for San Francisco, preparatory to leaving for the Atlantic States. Three years previously, I had entered Marysville, when it was a little town, built mostly of canvas. Distinctly did I recollect my feelings at that time. All those bright hopes and buoyant anticipations — how had they been realized? Alas! as are too many of the frail hopes of earth, they had been blasted and blighted in the bud. Now I left it a large city, containing ten thousand inhabitants. Blocks of brick, fire-proof buildings had been reared; churches also, whose spires seemed pointing to that better land; and school-houses, whose doors were thrown open to receive hundreds of happy children who had emigrated with their parents to this inland city. And I left it now, a sadder and a wiser woman; for there I had drunk deep draughts of sorrow, and had learned, by bitter experience, the fallacy of placing implicit confidence in earthly objects.

I was borne down those magnificent streams for the last time; yet every object is distinctly daguerreotyped in my mind as I saw it then. Yes! I bade all those scenes a final adieu; and would that I could have bade farewell to heart-troubles also. But how tenaciously they will gather around the fountain of memory, ever ready to spring to the surface, at the mention of some name, or half-forgotten word either of kindness or reproof! It was a bright May day, the last I passed in San Francisco. I met there several of the tried, firm friends of other days; and certainly I needed their support and protection then, if ever. Varying, conflicting emotions crowded so thick and fast upon the tablets of the brain, and so gained the ascendency over the power of self-control, that it was impossible for me to support my trembling frame without assistance, as I walked down the densely crowded wharf to get on board the steamer that was to convey me from scenes of suffering to my childhood's happy home.

That day, three steamers left that wharf, within an hour of each other, for the Atlantic States, — the "Uncle Sam," the "Panama," and the "Cortez." I went on board the "Uncle Sam." She was the last to leave, and was crowded with passengers: she had on board about eight hundred people.

When the gun was fired, — the signal for departure, — as the echo reverberated over the waters, I fancied it to be one unanimous farewell emanating from the breasts of all on board, — a farewell to the sunny vales and towering mountains, to the gold-studded placers and majestic streams, the deep ravines and rocky cañons, of beloved California.

What different emotions swelled the bosoms of

those persons who stood gazing, perhaps for the last time, on that great emporium of the West! Many perhaps, then on board, like myself, had threaded its sandy streets when in its state of infancy; had viewed the scene from Telegraph Hill, when nought but canvas shanties dotted the surface of those valleys, surrounded by numerous sand-hills, which had since been levelled to make room for elegant blocks of granite buildings, which reared their stately proportions, the admiration of thousands, and an honor to the energetic and enterprising projectors.

Some were returning, from a residence in that city and country, to their Eastern homes, blessed with an abundance of the shining metal which had lured them to its shores, and perhaps entirely destitute of all those principles of virtue and honesty that ever shed a brilliant lustre over the human mind, and give to the humble, indigent, and sorrow-stricken, a passport to a happy home above.

The possession of wealth does not necessarily pervert the human heart; and yet how often do we see the possessor utterly regardless of the feelings of the worthy poor! Wealth too often takes the precedence of intellect; and many times we have seen the gifted mind struggling through years of poverty, uncheered by even an encouraging word from the rich, and finally sink in obscurity into an early grave.

CHAPTER XXVI.

AFTER passing out at the Golden Gate, all three of the steamers were visible, each freighted with a rich cargo of human beings, and cleaving for themselves a pathway through the blue waters. The "Uncle Sam" and "Panama" were bound direct to Panama; the "Cortez" to San Juan.

The first night out on board a crowded steamer! Who that has experienced it can *ever* forget the confusion, the sea-sickness, the dissatisfaction reigning among room-mates, the squalling of parrots, the crying of babies, and all sorts of annoyances incident to the occasion?

For a person like myself, who was not sea-sick, and had no babies to worry about, and had only to enact the part of a silent spectator, the Babel-like confusion which reigned triumphant only served to divert my mind from my own sad thoughts, and I began to study the characters of my room-mates, through the science of physiognomy.

In our state-room, which opened upon the main deck, were three berths and a sofa. My ticket called for the sofa, which was a nice, soft, velvet one, and far preferable to a berth. My room-mates were an elderly lady, and her married daughter, who had a babe eight months old. Then there was an adopted daughter, about sixteen years of age, and a noisy parrot. This elderly lady also had a son on board, — a great, over-grown boy, who had taken a second-cabin passage, with the idea of lodging in the room with his mother.

The back of the sofa could be lifted up, so as to form a sort of shelf over the seat. This shelf, directly over the person who was lying upon the sofa, would be decidedly disagreeable and uncomfortable. The mother planned for that great boy to sleep upon this shelf, directly over me. To this I, of course, objected, knowing that he had a berth provided for him in the second cabin. Upon my objecting, the mother became determined that he *should* sleep there. I then appealed to the young man, asking him if he thought it would be very agreeable to lodge in a little state-room, with three ladies, a baby, and a parrot. He acknowledged it would not, and refused to comply with his mother's commands. Therefore, I got rid of him; which by no means ingratiated me into favor with the mother, who was very petulant indeed (owing to sea-sickness, I presume). But, after she ascertained that I would not be imposed upon, (if I were little,) she became quite affable, and lamented frequently that our tickets did not call for one and the same room on the Atlantic side.

The married daughter was a very lady-like, genteel sort of a person, totally dissimilar from her mother, and rather a victim to her (the mother's) dictatorial propensities. The adopted daughter was one of those good-natured, immovable sort of persons, always pleasant, yet doing about as she pleased, although receiving a severe reprimand every five minutes in the day from the old lady. The baby was a little darling, inheriting his mother's gentle disposition. The parrot was not a whit more quiet than its mistress. As soon as day began to break, he would begin to scream, after this fashion: " Come to breakfast;" " Six o'clock;" " Hot coffee;" " Mother! mother!" and such like expressions. If it was amusing at first, it soon became very annoying. There was one parrot on board so exceedingly profane and annoying, that its life was several times threatened by the passengers who roomed in close proximity to it. The woman to whom it belonged valued it above price. It could speak the English and Spanish languages quite *fluently*. It used to sit nights outside the woman's room. One morning, she missed its usual chatter, went upon deck, and it was nowhere to be found. Then what a time! Every one was ignorant as to its whereabouts; but a close observer might have detected a roguish twinkle lurking about the eyes of the mate of the ship, as he sympathized with the lady in her bereavement. Finally, the parrot was discovered, made fast to the mast-head of the ship. It was so frightened, it did not resume its usual chatter that day.

After we had been at sea a few days, the weather, which had been agreeably cool, changed to oppressive heat. The air in those little state-rooms was so confined and unhealthy, it behooved those who were able, to rise early in the morning, and go upon deck to inhale the balmy air. But, then, it was rather unpleasant to be hunted about as we were by the sailors, who were washing down the decks. We would perch ourselves upon something; and then, just as we were congratulating one another upon securing a nice seat, swash would come the water in torrents, compelling us to run for another seat, which would only afford us a similar temporary lodgment. If we escaped without getting our feet soaking wet, and our clothes somewhat draggled, we accounted ourselves fortunate in the extreme. After the expiration of a week, how the new faces began to appear! The decks began to get quite crowded. Some of them looked as if they had not been enjoying themselves very well while confined to their state-rooms. I had a great deal of sympathy for those afflicted with that disagreeable nausea; yet I often received kind wishes, to this effect: "How I do wish you could be sick, just for one hour! You would not look so smiling, if you felt as badly as I do." And yet I was forced to smile, when looking at their wo-begone countenances.

There were two or three female cabin passengers very sick with fever; and, oh, how they suffered, confined in a close state-room, with a raging fever consuming their very vitals!

One of the greatest sufferers was a lady who had been brought on board on a bed. She was dying of consumption. She was sick at home, and her physician had recommended a voyage to California. Thinking she might receive some benefit from a residence in that salubrious climate, her husband had taken her there. She had not remained there long, before she felt convinced that she must die.

Then she begged — oh, how earnestly! — to be taken home to see her darling babes once more. If she could be spared to clasp their little forms in one fond embrace, she could die happy. Her doom was sealed. Every day the hectic spot deepened upon that ethereal face; the racking cough increased in hollowness of sound; the fluctuating pulse grew fainter. She was fast hastening to "that bourne from whence no traveller returns."

The morning sun rose fair, but it shone upon a death-stamped countenance — upon loving lips forever silent — upon the cold hand which gave no returning pressure. She had passed away, with the names of her darlings upon her lips.

As the sun was sinking into the western waters, the steamer's course was stayed. The body of the devoted wife and loving mother was borne upon deck, covered by the American flag. Near by stood the bereaved husband, whose heart seemed wrung with the keenest sorrow. The stillness of death reigned on board that crowded steamer. In calm, serene accents, a minister of Christ breathed forth an earnest, heart-felt prayer; and the remains were launched into the bosom of the restless ocean. A splash, and all was over. The waves which had parted to receive that form of clay continued their ceaseless motion, and, by their ceaseless music, seemed to be chanting a requiem over the mother's grave, far, far down, among the coral dells and pearly caves of old ocean's unfathomed depths!

If the spirits of departed friends are conversant with our spirits, if they are indeed ministering angels to those whom they loved while in the flesh, the midnight slumbers of those motherless babes that night were blessed and sanctified by the seraphic presence of the beatified mother. In their infant dreams, it is the knowledge of her presence which causes those radiant smiles to flit across their fair, innocent faces.

Dear children! Many a tear of sympathy was dropped at the thought of their uncertain future, as the revolving wheels of the steamer carried us farther and farther from their mother's grave, which they could never look upon!

In a little while, all was gayety and mirth, bustle and confusion, singing and dancing, on board that floating structure. This being my first voyage after the eventful fiery one, my feelings were constantly agitated, thinking it possible a recurrence of those former scenes might be enacted. There were some on board who were acquainted with the history of my voyage out to California;

and they had repeated the story to their friends, until it had gained quite an extensive circulation among the ship's company.

One night, while seated in the door of my stateroom, I was very much amused at the remarks passed between two of the sailors, who were laying down hose upon the deck, as was the usual custom, as a precaution against fire. Says one, "Dick, what are you laying that extra hose for?" "Why," said he, "didn't you know there is a woman on board who never went to sea but what the ship she was on board of burnt before reaching her destination?" — "There isn't, though." — "Yes, there is; and I haven't the least idea the Uncle Sam will ever reach Panama." — "Have you seen her? How does she look?" — "I don't exactly know which one it is; but they say she looks just like any other woman." Thus the conversation continued for some time, to my great amusement. But the spell was broken; the startling cry of "Fire!" was not heard; and no event of importance occurred, by which the nerves of the most sensitive could be shocked.

We had two more burials at sea before reaching Panama. They were two firemen, who dropped dead while at their posts of duty, during the excessively hot weather.

CHAPTER XXVII.

After twelve days and some hours' sail from San Francisco, the old, walled city of Panama rose to view. The steamer's gun was fired; she dropped her anchor; and a fleet of boats and bungoes were seen approaching. They neared and surrounded the ship. Most or all of them were manned by swarthy-visaged, half-naked Carthaginians, and a mongrel race of natives, whose appearance and gestures were equally as repulsive.

Such a perfect Babel as that steamer's deck presented! Some running to and fro, looking for baggage, some bargaining and bantering with the boatmen, boatmen fighting with one another for a berth next the gangways, ladies screaming at the top of their voices, children bawling in unison, and parrots joining in the chorus! Curses and oaths, singing and shouting, filled up the intervals of this hurly-burly scene. I stood agape with astonishment at witnessing the haste and recklessness with which they rushed, helter-skelter, down the gangways, and tumbled (some of them headlong) into the boats. More than one individual I saw floundering in the water; and carpet-bags and valises were floating about quite merrily.

The hideous-looking boatmen kept up a continual jargon and fighting with one another; and perhaps, just as some person was going to step into a boat, some native would give it a shove away, and the person, pressed hard from behind, if not remarkably nimble, would get a ducking.

I was determined to wait until the last, rather than go with such a rush; and I did wait, until the coast was clear. Then our party, which consisted of four or five ladies and gentlemen, secured seats in a boat, and bade good bye to the Uncle Sam. We had gone but a short distance from the ship, when we heard the report of a gun booming over the water. The steamer Panama, which left in company with us, had arrived. She had about five hundred passengers on board; and, with the eight hundred who had just left the Uncle Sam, the hotels in Panama would be likely to be rather crowded. It behooved us to hasten, in order to secure a place on the floor, if nowhere else.

As we neared the shore, the water was full of natives, who waded off almost up to their necks, surrounded the boat, and arrested its progress. The boatmen are agreed with the natives on the shore to manage thus, in order to secure as many pieces of money as possible. No entreaties or threats could induce the boatmen to budge one inch nearer to the shore. There was no alternative but to place ourselves upon the backs of these natives, and (as the expression is) ride post-back to the shore. Before placing ourselves in this rather unladylike position, there was much screaming, and laughing, and crying, and scolding; but it all terminated in one general post-back ride to the shore. The natives being so submerged, one could not judge well of their muscular developments; and some of the more corpulent ladies were afraid to trust their immense proportions on the back of a slender native, for fear of being dropped. This accident did happen to some of them; and it was ever accompanied with much laughing and joking at the sufferer's expense. Finally, we were all landed, — some in one shape, and some in another. More than a dozen natives surrounded me, all holding their hands for a bit, (ten cents,) each claiming the honor of having carried me on his back to the shore. They all bore such a striking resemblance to one another, and having on no garments by which they could be distinguished, I was sorely troubled to know to whom I was indebted for my novel ride. It was settled, however, to their satisfaction.

The natives took our trunks upon their backs, (not us, this time,) and our party started for the Louisiana Hotel. When we arrived there, it was literally jammed full; but, knowing we should fare no better by going elsewhere, we crowded ourselves in with the multitude.

This was in the afternoon, and our appetites were considerably sharpened by the rather scantily furnished tables which had been spread on board the steamer for one or two days previous to our arrival.

Six or seven of us ladies were shown to a room on the second floor, which overlooked the court-yard in the centre of the range of buildings. Each story was surrounded by a balcony. Our room had no windows, but two very extensive doors, which opened like folding-doors on to the balcony. The partitions all through the house only ran two thirds of the height to the ceiling; so there was plenty of ventilation and plenty of noise circulating through the house. There was not a particle of paint or paper in the whole building. The walls and partitions were of rough boards, and these were all whitewashed. The great vaulted passages leading through the house, and the great wide, worn staircases, presented a cheerless and gloomy aspect. In our room were six or seven cots, over which were thrown two sheets and a straw pillow to each cot. This constituted the entire stock of furniture, if we except two old rickety chairs and our trunks.

From the balcony opposite our door we could watch the proceedings in the cook-room; and it was amusing to watch those half-naked natives knock over the fowl, of which there were numbers in the back yard, about half-divest them of their feathers, hurry them into a kettle, and by the time they were well heated through, run with them to the tables, if they were not met on the way there by the half-famished passengers, who would snatch the half-cooked viands from their hands, and beat a hasty retreat to their rooms.

In vain we waited to be summoned to supper. Finally, one of our party made a descent upon the cooks, and procured the wherewith to appease, in a measure, our hunger.

The Uncle Sam's passengers had intended to get mules, and start that night from Panama to cross the isthmus; and this could have been accomplished, had not the natives been so shrewd. When they saw the steamer Panama coming in directly after the Uncle Sam, they rightly conjectured, that, if they kept their mules out of sight until all from both steamers were landed, there would be such a demand for mules they could get any price they saw fit to ask. Therefore, when mules were called for by those of the passengers who reached the shore first, there were none to be found. No entreaty or persuasion could induce them to bring one forward; but we were told there would be plenty on the morrow. That afternoon a party of us took a stroll around the city, visited the oldest and largest cathedral in the place, walked upon the battlements which surround this ancient and once flourishing city, but now, in many places, wearing the aspect of decay and ruin. Some portions of the wall were falling into ruins; but in some places it was sufficiently wide for two carriages to drive abreast; but there were no vehicles there then. There were the sentry-boxes, built at short intervals along the battlements, which, in days gone by, had sheltered the wearied sentinel during his nightly patrol.

I saw in some places the ruins of old churches and convents. Some portions of the high stone walls would be standing, out of the sides of which were growing bushes and small trees. The sight of those trees growing out of high stone walls at once attracted my attention. For how many ages must those old walls have been exposed to burning suns and deluging rains, to have thus afforded sustenance for those scraggy shrubs and trees! The stones were all moss-grown, and rank vines were running in great profusion over the decaying ruins. An air of silent desertion seemed to pervade those ruinous remains, which gave rise to melancholy reflections. They forcibly reminded one of the mutability of all things earthly. Just as the setting sun was casting its red beams upon the high and narrow stained-glass windows of the rich old cathedral, we were wandering under its vaulted roof, feasting our astonished senses with a sight of the massive gold and silver ornaments which were displayed in such rich profusion upon the walls. What an air of mystery and gloom seemed to surround us! How our voices echoed and reverberated in the far-off niches and recesses of this gloomy-looking edifice. Several times I was startled by the appearance of some old monk, with his cowl closely drawn, who would start from some niche in the wall, where he had remained unperceived, and, without uttering a word, hold out a silver plate, whereupon you were expected to deposit a piece of money. When once more in the open air, I experienced a sense of freedom from the feelings of mystery and gloom, which unavoidably cluster around one while traversing those silent cathedrals.

We then repaired to the vestibule of a convent, not with the expectation of gaining admittance, however. There was a wooden frame which turned in the wall, after the manner of those yard-gates which turn upon a pivot, and on which stood a pitcher of water and a glass. After drinking, a person is expected to leave a piece of money beside the pitcher. Every few moments, this frame is turned by an unseen hand; but, when the pitcher and glass appear again, the money, if there had been any beside it, had disappeared.

It being a moonlight evening, several of us ladies, accompanied by one gentleman, started to prosecute our walk through some other parts of the city. We passed through several streets, or, as they appeared to me, lanes; but they looked *so* gloomy! And, then, those old ruins seemed such grand lurking-places for the revengeful Spaniard, with his murderous stiletto, that we all frightened ourselves by such imaginings, and ran back again to the hotel as quickly as possible.

What a night was that at Panama! So many

returning Californians, and some such wild ones, too! They seemed determined to make night hideous with their singing and shouting. There was little sleep for any one in Panama that night.

CHAPTER XXVIII.

As soon as daylight dawned, the natives began to swarm in the streets with their mules, opposite to the hotels, and the people commenced bargaining for the use of them.

The railroad was completed from Aspinwall to within eighteen miles of Panama. Eighteen miles! When we came to traverse the route, it seemed thirty, at least. As the rains had commenced, we were advised to travel the Cruces route, as the Gorgorna route would be impassable on account of the mud.

Some of the passengers who had before traversed the Cruces route advised all the ladies to dispense with the side-saddle altogether, as it would be utterly impossible for them to retain their seats, unless upon the gentleman's Spanish saddle. Most of us were provided with India-rubber boots, and pants, and a large sombrero, as a protection for our heads.

The natives asked twenty dollars for the use of a good, plump-looking mule, to take us to Obispo, at which place was the terminus of the railroad; but one could get a miserable-looking animal, which, in all probability, would die on the way, and leave you to prosecute the remainder of your journey on foot, for twelve and fifteen dollars. For my mule I paid twenty; and, many times during the journey, I had occasion to congratulate myself for having secured such a gentle, kind, serviceable little animal. I really became so attached to him during the journey, that I parted from him with regret. Generally, the natives from whom you hire your mules, and pay for them in advance, trot along with the company, and are ready, upon your arrival, to take the animal.

There was great frolicking and laughing with the ladies while fixing away on the mules. I shall never forget *my* feelings when I found myself seated astride my mule, arrayed in boots and pants, with my feet firmly planted in the stirrups, ready for any emergency.

About five o'clock in the morning, I left the hotel, in company with thirty or more of the passengers. They all travelled in parties of thirty and forty together. Most of the children were carried across by the natives. They were seated astride their necks, with their little hands clasped across the natives' foreheads; while they have hold of the children's legs in front. Those who have infants generally get some gentleman to take them in front of him on the saddle.

One of our passengers (a widow lady, with two little children) was very sick indeed when she arrived at Panama. She was advised to remain there for the present; but, although she felt convinced that her days on earth were numbered, she preferred to go on with the company. She was placed in a hammock: each of her little children (one twelve months, and the other three years) were carried on the backs of natives, who walked by her side.

When only six miles out from Panama, she breathed her last-drawn sigh. They stopped, dug a grave for the mother by the lonely way-side, and deposited her remains therein. It was a sad spectacle. Well was it for those little orphans that their extreme youth prevented them from realizing the extent of their affliction.

A kind-hearted woman — although the roughest-looking one in the company — volunteered to take charge of the babes until they arrived in New York. Upon arriving at Obispo, a collection of two hundred dollars was taken for the children. Often, since, I have thought of that lonely grave by the way-side, with no stone, or even board, to mark the spot, and upon which no tear of affection will ever fall. She buried her husband in San Francisco, three weeks previous to her departure for the Atlantic States. She was getting home by charity; and, being a delicate, feeble woman, could not endure the fatigue of the journey. Deep-seated sorrow had sapped the fountains of life, and she died among strangers, far from friends and home.

Two others of our number died, and were buried on the way. One was a gentleman whose mule had died, and he was footing it along, when he suddenly fell, and expired. Probably his death was caused by disease of the heart. One steerage passenger, who was walking across, died from overheating himself.

For the distance of six miles, our route lay over a good, paved road, and we galloped along, exceedingly delighted with the scenery, our mules, and the good road. "If this is crossing the Isthmus," said one, "I shall never believe again the horrid accounts I have heard respecting the trip;" but, before the termination of the journey, she thought the one-half had not been told. Soon the road became more rugged, and we began to enter the rocky defiles, ascend the steep mountain passes, and descend into dark, rocky ravines. The sun, which had been shining with tropical fervency, now withdrew his rays, and the rain descended in torrents. The deafening thunder seemed to shake those old mountains to their very base. In an instant we were soaking wet; for, oh, how it did pour! In a short time it was over, and the sun shining bright and hot as ever. Two such showers as this we encountered during that mule-back trip.

The scenery through the mountains almost defies description. There are defiles through the solid rock, so narrow as to admit only one mule at a time; while, on each side, the rocks rise to the height of fifteen, twenty, and, in some places, thirty feet. These rocks are surmounted by tall trees, whose dense foliage, blending overhead, completely excludes the sight of the blue sky above.

Sometimes these narrow passes are so descending, as to render it almost impossible to retain your seat upon the mule. In some places there are regular stepping-stones, into each of which little

little holes have been worn by the mules' feet, that so many times, and oft, have traversed those dangerous passes. I could compare the descent to nought but placing a mule at the top of a flight of stairs, getting upon his back, and riding down.

Those mules are so careful and sure-footed, and so well accustomed to travelling through those frightful places, that there is no necessity whatever of guiding them. You have only to place the bridle over the pommel of the saddle, (those Spanish saddles have a high pommel in front,) and look out for yourself. In descending, we were obliged to lean far back on the animal's back, and grasp the crupper with all our might. It seemed as if our safety depended solely upon the strength of the crupper. How I cried sometimes, with fright! but then I was careful not to let any one see me, and generally took the time for such ebullition of feeling when it was raining hard, and the water would unavoidably be coursing down my face.

How careful those mules were! That day I learned to love them. In going down those rocky flights, they would hold their heads low down, then put one foot over and plant it firmly in one of those little holes, then the other in the same way, then bring their hind feet on to the same shelf, then go down on to another, and so on to the bottom. Then perhaps commence, and make an ascent equally as toilsome. They have nothing to eat or drink on the way, and never once attempt to nip the herbage that grows, in some places, by the way-side.

Once, as there were about fifty mules all in a line, ascending one of those steep mountain passes, the one in advance, which was laden with three large trunks, made a misstep, and fell. These animals are so sure-footed that they never stumble except when giving out, and never fall, unless to die. This one was very weak, and failing fast, but might have succeeded in reaching the top of this dangerous pass, had not the trunks swayed on one side, and hit the rocks, thereby causing him to fall. When passing up those rocky flights, it is utterly impossible for a mule to step backwards, off one of those shelves, without falling, and as utterly impossible to turn the mule about, on account of the extreme narrowness of the way. The fallen mule, in making desperate attempts to rise with those heavy trunks lashed to him, as a natural consequence kept falling back, thereby crowding hard upon those behind him. I was seated on the fifth mule in the rear of the fallen one. Such a shouting and bawling as there was with the natives, who were trying to disencumber the poor beast of the trunks, and, at the same, prevent him from throwing himself any farther back, as, by so doing, he would endanger the lives of those behind him.

How firmly my little mule planted his feet upon the shelf he was on, rounded himself into as small a compass as possible, and awaited his fate. He seemed to comprehend the whole; and, by his looks, I fancied he said, as a token of assurance to me, "I will die here rather than take one step backwards." Finally they disengaged the trunks from the animal, and hoisted them up on to the banks above. As the mule was evidently dying, they cut his throat, and lifted him up also. This scene detained us more than an hour; for those natives seemed to make no progress towards extricating the mule from his painful position, but were running to and fro, bawling at the top of their voices, hunting ropes, and ordering one another. The passengers who were far behind were calling loudly to know what was the cause of the detention. Some were cursing the tardy natives; the women were crying with fear; and, if a daguerreotype view could have been taken of the scene, I think it would have had a tendency to deter some from ever crossing the Isthmus of Darien on muleback.

Upon entering one of those defiles, the natives who are on foot (and there are generally quite a number with each party) go in advance, and keep up a loud shouting, to prevent any party which may be coming in an opposite direction from entering, as it would be death to one or other of the parties' mules, should they meet. We occasionally passed over the carcasses of mules in these places, which had been killed to afford others a passage. We were so fearful that the natives would not make noise enough, that we joined in the shouting, and felt truly grateful when we emerged from the bowels of the earth.

The day previous to our arrival at Panama, the steamer Illinois arrived at Aspinwall, with a load of passengers from New York for California. In crossing, we all met at different points on the way.

Sometimes, upon arriving at a defile, we would hear a loud shouting within; then we would halt, rein our mules out on each side of the way, and await their egress. Some, upon emerging from the defile, looked very much jaded and fatigued; others were laughing and joking. How earnestly we eyed them, as they appeared one after another, thinking perhaps we might see some friend or acquaintance from home.

Upon thus meeting, each party would accost the other with all the freedom and familiarity of old acquaintances; and some of the remarks which were passed were really laughable. Upon the back of one mule were seated two persons, a young man and an elderly woman. At sight of them, some of the gentlemen of our party hurrahed, which was answered by the woman with a wave of her calash, (she wore one of those large old-fashioned green ones,) and a "Hurrah for California!" "That is right," said one, addressing the young man, "take your mother with you; if we had, we might have been spared much suffering." And thus they joked. Some who had been rather unsuccessful advised the emigrants to turn back, even then. "Why?" said they, "is there not plenty of gold in California?" "Yes, there is gold enough; but you may not be lucky enough to get any of it."

They gave us no encouragement as to the route over which they had passed. All said, "Expect to find it as bad and worse than you can possibly conceive of." This was disheartening, I assure you.

Sometimes the trail would be quite passable, and then one could enjoy the scenery. The tropical foliage is beautiful; and among the leaves and branches were hopping birds of beautiful plumage, rendering the woods vocal with their sweetest songs. Monkeys and parrots we saw in abundance.

On the way we passed several hotels, — nothing more than canvas shanties, with large signs attached, bearing the appellations of "Astor House," "St. Charles Hotel," "Revere House," etc. They were kept by Americans, and at them one could procure plenty of fruit and liquors of all kinds; but the wise ones were very abstemious, as a great deal of the sickness on the isthmus is engendered by eating and drinking to excess in a climate so excessively warm.

Oh, how tired we grew! and yet, at every hotel, the distance seemed to increase rather than decrease.

Upon first entering the forests on the isthmus, my attention was directed to what looked like ropes hanging from the trees. I soon found them to be vines that had run up on the trees, out on the branches, and were suspended therefrom in every direction. They were leafless, and the color of a rope.

We crossed the Chagres River once only before

reaching Obispo. How dark and deep it looked, as we were going down a steep declivity directly into it! We were assured it was quite shallow, and not dangerous to ford; and that, if we allowed our mules to take their own course, we should be carried safely across.

One young lady from Marysville was very much frightened, and kept constantly asserting that she should be drowned, she knew. Upon reaching the brink of the river, she suddenly reined in her mule, just as he was going to step in. He became offended at such treatment, and shook her off plump into the river. Such a screaming! You would have thought a dozen women were in the river. She was brought out, and placed again upon her mule, with instructions how to proceed, and was carried safely over. The water was not up to our stirrups, in the deepest place; but it looked black and deep, down in that dark ravine. I breathed more freely when safely across.

Once we came to a little slough, over which was built a narrow bridge of poles. I happened to be ahead at that place, and called to know whether I should cross the bridge, or follow the trail through the slough, which looked very miry. They told me to let the mule act his own pleasure. He first tried the strength of the bridge by placing his foot upon it, and feeling all about, as far as he could reach; then he turned, and went down the trail to the slough, and there reconnoitred in the same way; then he turned to the bridge again. I concluded he thought that the safest way of crossing. Upon reaching it, he stopped, made one leap, and cleared it at a bound, and came very near clearing himself of me, too. I was wholly unprepared for such an emergency, and came very near losing my equilibrium. All the other mules came leaping over except one, which, I expect, was so far gone, he could not jump. He stepped upon the bridge: it broke beneath his weight, and he fell. The lady was thrown from his back; and, altogether, there was quite a scene.

After this, we met two gentlemen on mule-back, and of them we inquired the distance to Obispo. The reply from one was, "I should think it was a dozen miles, and the very worst road you ever travelled."—"Oh, no," said the other, "not so bad as that. This is the gentleman's first trip to California. When he has crossed the Isthmus two or three times, he will not get so quickly discouraged. It is about two miles to Obispo; and rather a rough road, to be sure, but not worse than you have passed, I presume." How those cheering words revived my drooping spirits! I felt (and every lady of the company, I presume, felt the same) as if I could not retain my seat upon my mule but a little longer. Every part of my body ached so hard, I could not tell where the pain was most severe. If I had been placed upon the rack, and every joint drawn asunder, I could not have been much lamer or sorer than I then was.

It was two o'clock in the afternoon, and we had been riding since five in the morning, without once leaving our mules, over a road which, for its rugged, uneven, and dangerous passes, beggars description.

Suddenly we heard the shrill whistle of a steam engine. Our lagging spirits revived. We toiled on, and reached the top of an eminence which overlooked the beautiful valley of Obispo; and there, far below us, we beheld a scene calculated to inspire the most despondent with renewed hope and courage. There was the terminus of the railroad; and on the track were twelve long cars, headed by an engine, which was puffing and blowing, and sending forth whistle after whistle, long, loud, and clear, its echoes awakening the hitherto unbroken solitude of the primeval forests of New Granada.

Those of the company who had sufficient life and strength remaining to make any demonstration of joy, did so. As we descended the mountain, we were perceived, and welcomed by firing of cannon and loud cheering.

Several hundred United States troops had arrived there, *en route* for California. They were all out on the plaza. Four or five large American flags were floating upon the breeze from the roofs of large temporary hotels which had been erected along the line of the railroad; and, as fast as the road progressed, they were transported along to the terminus. Here I saw a railroad for the first time since leaving Baltimore, a lapse of four years.

When we arrived in the valley, and halted in front of the depot, I suppose our forlorn, jaded appearance excited the sympathy of those there assembled, for many stepped forward to assist us in dismounting. They lifted us from our saddles, and placed us, not upon our feet, — for not one of the ladies in the company could stand, — but flat upon the ground in the mud.

One lady in particular — who rode nearly the whole way, holding her babe on the saddle in front of her — fainted, the moment they lifted her from her mule, and it was a long time before she recovered her consciousness.

Upon leaving Panama, she had consigned it to the care of a gentleman, who was going to take it across the Isthmus on the saddle with himself; but whose mule gave out, and fell with him. In endeavoring to save the infant from injury, he received several severe contusions on his back and head, from the effects of which he did not recover during the journey to New York. This so frightened the mother, that she took the babe herself; and, in consequence of thus exerting her strength to take care of herself and child, — when those who had no child to attend to could scarcely retain their seats, — she came very near dying.

After remaining a few moments in the mud, I made an attempt to walk. I would go a few steps, and then fall; pick myself up again, take a few more steps, and then tumble the other way. I attributed my inability to walk partly to my Indiarubber boots slipping on the muddy ground, and partly to the benumbed and stiffened state of my limbs. While I was thus staggering about in the vain endeavor to reach a hotel, a gentleman came along, picked me up, and carried me to the desired haven.

CHAPTER XXIX.

Cars were in readiness to take us immediately to Aspinwall, where the steamer North Star was waiting to convey us to New York. Many of the gentlemen took passage in them; but the ladies were too exhausted to think of proceeding farther that day; and, as the specie and baggage had not all arrived, there was no danger of the North Star sailing until the next night.

So we all retired, and did not rise again until the next morning. Our accommodations at Obispo were similar to those at Panama — great rush, nothing to eat, and not much to lie upon.

In the morning, as we were well-nigh famished, a gentleman of the party invited a friend of mine and myself to breakfast with him, as he had been to the trouble of purchasing something, and hiring it cooked expressly for himself. The breakfast consisted of broiled chicken, fried plantains, and eggs. That meal cost five dollars, and it was the only one I had while at Obispo. That forenoon, our baggage arrived, and, while out on the plaza, it was exposed to one of the hardest showers I ever witnessed. Wo to the contents of those trunks which were not water-proof!

I must not leave the beautiful valley of Obispo without descanting upon its loveliness. It was inclosed by lofty hills, whose sides and summits were clothed with the most beautiful tropical foliage. There grew the tall palm-tree, laden with its milky fruit; the luscious pine-apple; also bananas, and plantains in abundance.

There were, perhaps, twenty native bamboo-huts, thatched with the woven fibre of the palm-leaf, scattered about the valley; around the doors of which, and under the leafy shade of the lime and palmetto, lounged the indolent natives, of both sexes. And why should they exert themselves, when nature has so abundantly supplied their wants?

They appeared perfectly happy and contented in their ignorance. No soaring aspirations for fame caused them to pass sleepless nights and anxious days. They were slaves to no goddess of fashion; and, if they had any pride, I cannot conceive to what point it tended, unless it was an overweening desire to excel in roasting monkeys. Oh, this was a sunny spot! I can see it, even now, in my mind's eye, as it appeared when viewed from the top of that mountain height, after a day of toilsome travel. That old adage, "It is always the darkest just before day," was never more fully illustrated than when, after such a toilsome, dangerous day's ride as we had accomplished, that lovely, pleasant valley burst upon our view. That last two miles of mule-back travel I shall never forget. Whether it surpassed all other portions of the route in steep and dangerous passes, or whether we were so completely worn out with fatigue, that everything appeared more dark and gloomy than it really was, I cannot say; but that old maxim kept ringing in my ears, and cheering me on—"It is always the darkest just before day." And, certainly, I could not compare that sunshiny valley, at the terminus of our route, to other than the brightest day that ever followed the darkest night.

About four o'clock in the afternoon, we seated ourselves in the cars bound to Aspinwall. Those cars on the Isthmus had cane seats and backs, and were, therefore, not so comfortable for the sick, sore, and lame, as if they had been otherwise.

We were borne over the track quite slowly, as the many short curves which the road made prevented their going with greater speed. The railroad seemed to follow the bed of the Chagres River.

We crossed it several times. The scenery was grand and sublime, commingled with the beautiful. On one side of the track, perhaps, a towering mountain raised its rocky sides far above us; while, on the opposite side, the eye might wander far, far down a steep precipice, causing a shudder to run through the frame at the thought of an accident occurring at such a spot.

How frightened the parrots, paroquets, and monkeys, must have been, when the iron horse first startled those leafy solitudes with his fiery snort! Never again will profound stillness reign triumphant along the course of the Chagres River. Those feathered songsters, of brilliant plumage, lured to its vine-clad banks by the gentle ripple of its tiny waves, will fly, startled from their leafy coverts, at the approach of the iron steed.

By and by, the town of Aspinwall appeared to view. The country all about looked so sunken and marshy, as to impress the beholder at once with an idea of its unhealthy location. It was quite a place, however, and at that time seemed to be all alive with people. We passed from the cars directly on board the steamer, as it was near night, and we wished to get possession of our rooms before sailing. I ascertained the steamer would not get away before midnight, as it was an almost endless task to select the baggage, and get it on board.

Being very weary, I concluded to lie down, and get a nap in the first part of the evening, in order to be awake, and be on deck, when we left Aspinwall.

When next I opened my eyes, it was broad daylight. Aspinwall was far out of sight, and we on the broad Atlantic.

Amid all the bustle and confusion preparatory to sailing, even firing of guns, I had slept soundly. One lady, thinking I would like to see Aspinwall by lamp-light, endeavored to awaken me; said she spoke my name several times, and shook my arm, but still I slept on; and she left me to the enjoyment of my dreams.

Upon going on deck, I met again all the Uncle Sam's passengers, and saw many strangers who had come on board at Aspinwall. On the North Star I had only two room-mates, and was minus baby and parrot.

Now that I was on the Atlantic, I felt that the distance between home and myself would be speedily annihilated. Nothing occurred worthy of note during the passage; and, on the ninth day after leaving Aspinwall, we made Sandy Hook. It is impossible to describe my sensations upon nearing my native land, after an absence of four years. I was returning *alone*, too, to the home of my youth. At times, my feelings were overpowering.

When the health officer boarded us, I saw a sight that would have drawn pity from the breast of the most obdurate. It appeared that at Aspinwall there had been brought on board, and placed in the steerage, three sick individuals, the remnant of a family of eight persons, who had left New York for California a short time previous. On their arrival at the Isthmus, the father and mother had sickened, and died. The six children started to cross to Panama. They were robbed of all their money on the way; and, ere they arrived at Panama, the two eldest brothers and one sister died, leaving a young brother and two sisters, penniless and sick. In this condition they were found by some good Samaritan, brought back to Aspinwall, and placed on board the North Star. They were very sick indeed — in fact, but just alive; but their sickness was not of an infectious nature.

While preparations were being made to lower away a boat in which to take them to the hospital, they were brought aft, and placed upon deck. One look at those poor, sick, emaciated children of sorrow would so stamp itself upon the pages of memory, that long afterwards their ghastly countenances, with their sunken, hollow eyes, ashen lips, and shrivelled forms, would present themselves in your day-dreams as well as your night.

The eldest girl was about sixteen; the other might be fourteen, and the boy twelve. Not two months since, they had left New York, a healthy, happy family. Now the remaining three were brought back to die in the hospital. The eldest girl died in the boat while being transported to the hospital. The other two, I have no doubt, quickly followed her, as they looked more like tenants of the tomb than aught else.

I must not forget to mention the fate of those two little orphans whose mother was buried on the Isthmus. The kind-hearted lady who took them in charge had faithfully fulfilled her mission. The children were well and happy, in their guileless innocence. A collection was taken for them on board the North Star, to the amount of three hundred dollars. This, added to the two hundred previously taken, was delivered up to the lady who had them in charge; and she was going with them to Cincinnati, at which place a sister of the deceased mother resided, and to whom the dying mother had bequeathed them.

CHAPTER XXX.

We neared the city of New York. Soon its domes, turrets, and spires, became more distinct. We were fast nearing home. Home! How the mention of that word sent a thrill to my heart! It is scarcely possible to describe my feelings at that time; exuberant joy, mingled with sorrowful reminiscences which came crowding thick and fast over the ocean of memory, overshadowing all the bright hopes and sunny feelings of the heart.

We reached the wharf late in the afternoon. It is needless to describe the bustle incident to the arrival of an ocean steamer, crowded with passengers. It is enough to say, that after being jammed, and jostled, and crushed, to your infinite satisfaction, you find yourself on board a hack, bound to one of the many hotels which intersperse the city.

The next day, I was too sick to start for home, completely prostrated by excitement, I suppose. The next day, I left New York. The following morning, I neared my native town. The station was reached; I left the cars. I had purposely kept my arrival secret, the better to take them by surprise.

In returning, after a long absence, to the home of our youth, we often find ourselves disappointed. A part of the brightness is almost sure to have passed away. Our eyes are changed, even if the things we look upon remain the same. The persons we have loved too are sure to have altered, and rarely for the better; for, if they be still on the bright side of life, the rose-bud is generally more beautiful than the rose; and, if they be on the autumnal side of the hill, we shall have to mark many a leaf that has fallen, many a flower that has faded away.

CHAPTER XXXI.

Before laying aside my pen, I am constrained to say a word regarding the moral tone of society as it existed in California as early as the years 1851 and 1852.

Recollect, kind reader, that the state of society in California at the present day is as unlike what it was at the time alluded to above as are the golden tints of the eastern sky ere the glorious orb of day bursts upon the view, and the dark, portentous gloom which overspreads the horizon, presaging a coming storm.

To what cause could be attributed this lack of morality, which seemed to pervade the greater portion of the community at that early day, and which necessarily dimmed the lustre of the brightest gem in God's magnificent footstool? Was it the atmospheric influence which surrounded them? or were the evil propensities of their natures more forcibly displayed for the very reason that they felt themselves beyond the reach of all those conventional forms of society which, in our puritanical country, serve to restrain, more or less, the inherent evil of our natures?

Travellers who have wandered in the sunny regions of a tropical clime, and have mingled with the inhabitants, can scarcely fail to perceive the effect of that balmy, blissful atmosphere upon the human passions. Their quick, impulsive natures, warm and generous hearts, overflowing with love and affection; the bewitching naiveté of manner so characteristic of the females has often proved a theme for the poet and historian.

California, although not situated within the tropics, many of its sunny vales possess all the characteristics of soil and climate, and afford to one all the delights pertaining to a residence in those genial climes, and, at the time to which I refer, many of those captivating females had found a home within its borders.

It is oftentimes the case that persons naturally pure, and possessed of good principles, by constant intercourse with those whose nationalities are less stringent with regard to morality, are almost unconsciously, as it were, led to adopt customs, and imbibe sentiments that at first were quite revolting to their natures.

Ever willing to place the best construction upon another's conduct, I would much rather infer that all of the evil which displays itself is the result of a vacillating mind, unable to withstand temptation, rather than of an innate desire to set at defiance the laws of God and man.

Persons from all classes were to be found in California, — the moral and the immoral, the tempter and the tempted. Well may it call a blush to the cheek of our own sex, when I assert that the immoral predominated, as far as the female portion of the community were concerned. I have been an unwilling observer of transactions, which, had they been related to me, would have shaken my opinion somewhat respecting the veracity of the narrator. Think of a town in California where the females numbered more than two hundred, and from that number the pure, high-minded, and virtuous could not have selected more than three or four with whom they could have associated, and have derived a sweet pleasure in the interchange of all those ennobling sentiments which shed such a halo of loveliness around fair woman's shrine.

Now, it is characteristic of my humble self to illustrate every subject by relating some event which has come under my personal observation, and which will, I think, serve to interest.

Among the first who emigrated from the city of Boston to the western El Dorado were a mother and daughter.

The daughter, yet scarcely fifteen years of age, gave promise of extreme loveliness. Carefully had that mother guarded her, lest a too early acquaintance with the chilling realities of life should rob her young and guileless heart of a portion of its pristine purity and undimmed faith.

Of that mother's early history but little was known; yet it was often whispered by the gossiping ones that the remembrance of her own sad, youthful experience had given that shade of melancholy, that tinge of sadness, which at times shaded so deeply her yet fair brow. Whatever had been her bitter trials and disappointments, it was evident to a casual observer that the whole wealth of her affections, the deep, unfathomable love of a mother's heart were centred on the well-being of her only child.

The better to acquire a competency, wherewith to surround the loved one with all those appliances of comfort so desirable to a young and beautiful girl, the mother determined to seek a home within the precincts of the "Golden State." Better, far better, had she immured herself and child in the catacombs of Rome than thus to have launched their frail bark upon the golden wave of a California sea.

The most ambitious votary of admiration there at that time must have been satisfied, and even satiated, with the amount of homage, adulation, and heartless flattery, which was poured into their too willing ears. One can realize the danger likely to be incurred by placing a young, lovely, and attractive female in a country where virtue was regarded by the mass only as a name, and while she was yet too young to discriminate between the respectful homage of sensible gentlemen and the soul-sickening, hypocritical, despicable flatteries which often flow so smoothly from under the moustache of the soulless, " vanity-puffed, shallow-brained apology." for a man. One saw many of those specimens in a day's walk through the city of San Francisco, and also in her sister cities.

Nightly they would convene in those gilded halls of iniquity, and pursue their soul-killing avocation. To be sure, they nightly won their thousands, little caring for the mental agony of their victims, whom they had robbed of the last ounce of dust, which they had been months, perhaps, accumulating, and which they had intended to have transmitted to their families in their far distant homes. Wait patiently, wife and little ones, — wait patiently for the father and husband to learn the best and most effective lesson ever taught by that inexorable schoolmaster, experience! If his first lesson is severe indeed, as a general thing, he is not over anxious to risk a second recital, and the absent wife may hope again to welcome his loved image to the now sorrowful home.

These professed gamblers are never content with ruining those of their own sex, but are ever on the alert and the watch for victims from among the youthful, unsophisticated, and beautiful of the opposite sex; and Lillie Lee was far too captivating to remain long in obscurity.

Notwithstanding the vigilance of her mother, she had formed an acquaintance with one of the most enticing of the gambling brotherhood. For weeks and months he had been gradually gaining a strong foothold upon her affections, by practising all those insidious arts which too often successfully entrap the uninitiated. He knew he was beloved, and, knowing that, felt secure of his victim.

The affection bestowed upon that dissolute gamester was deserving a better object. Upon the promise of a speedy marriage, she left her mother's roof; and together they fled to one of the interior towns.

Who can graphically describe that mother's anguish, upon learning the flight of her darling? Within a few hours of their departure, the bereaved, heart-broken, and nearly frantic woman was on the track of the seducer and his victim. She arrived about midnight at the town where the fugitives had taken up their abode. After travelling nearly thirty-six hours without once tasting food, or taking any rest, this grief-stricken woman procured a suitable disguise, and, arming herself with a "Colt's revolver," started on her mission of death.

Grief had rendered her frantic, and, in the desperation of the moment, she had made a vow, and registered it on the tablet of a broken heart, that she would avenge her daughter's ruin by taking the life of her seducer; forgetting, in the frenzy of excitement, that she was assuming a power never intended to be usurped by the sinful children of earth.

She threaded her lonely way through the nearly deserted streets of that inland city, never wavering in her murderous intentions, until she paused at the entrance of one of those brilliantly lighted gambling-saloons which spread their contaminating influence on all around. She entered, expecting and hoping to find the object of pursuit engaged in his nefarious vocation. She saw, however, only the usual appurtenances of these houses of sin. Elegantly attired women, within whose natures long since had expired the last flickering spark of feminine modesty, were seated, dealing cards at a game of Faro or Lansquenet, and, by their winning smile and enticing manner, inducing hundreds of men to stake their all upon their tables. The stricken mother passed through the crowd, but could nowhere see the object of her search.

In this manner she visited all the houses of like reputation, with similar success. By some means or other, she obtained a clue to their whereabouts, reached the door of their room, and, in a disguised voice, demanded admittance. After a long delay, the door was opened, and the despoiled and despoiler met face to face. Quicker than thought, the revolver was levelled at his breast, when a piercing shriek broke on the stillness of the night, and the words, "Mother! oh, mother! in Heaven's name, desist!" burst, in tones of concentrated anguish, from the affrighted girl. In an instant she had thrown herself between the parties, and was imploring her mother to spare the life of him she loved.

What power had changed that mother's anger to grief too deep for utterance? Was it the vivid recollection of a similar scene, enacted long, long ago, in which she had participated? Did the form of her kind and sainted mother rise before her? Yes; she beheld again, in fancy, that calm, sad face, the memory of which had often disturbed her midnight slumbers. These harrowing recollections of the would-be-forgotten past were quite too overpowering. It was long before she was restored to consciousness; and not until repeatedly assured by that deeply dyed villain, that he would make ample restitution by marrying her daughter, could she be persuaded to return to her hotel. The earnest pleadings of the mother could not induce the infatuated girl to separate from her lover. The mother returned to San Francisco.

Months flew by, scarcely heeded by the happy child. The long-deferred marriage proved no source of grief to her. She *loved*, and was happy. She had so much confidence in his honor, that she felt certain he would marry her. Honor! what a desecration of the word, when used in connection with such a fiend in human shape!

Perhaps he would have married her, — for he seemed happy only when in her presence, — if he had not been indissolubly bound to another. Lillie had yet to learn that stunning truth. It must be so; yet how he trembled, and shrank from making a disclosure, which, he well knew, would chill the very life-blood in her veins!

The wife of his youth, tired of living alone in her distant home, had formed the determination to join her husband, and follow his fortunes in the "Golden Empire." Her decision was irrevocable. Even the time was appointed when he should meet her at the bay. He felt, at times, like flying with Lillie to parts unknown; for, depraved as he was, she, by her artless, winning ways, and rich wealth of affection, had stirred the long-dormant fountain of love in his bosom. Yes, now was coming his hour of retribution; for he loved Lillie, and must leave her to the fate that almost always attends the deeply erring. Time was pressing; he must reveal all. It was done; and for hours she sat like one petrified. She could only articulate, "Mother! mother! receive again your heart-broken child!"

They left, that day, for San Francisco, — he, to meet his injured, unloved wife; she, to be received in the arms of her wronged, but still loving mother. Under the influence of a powerful narcotic, which had been administered at her own option, she was conveyed to her mother's house; and there we will leave her for the present.

Behold how majestically that mammoth ocean steamer cuts her way through the sparkling waters of the bay! Now she gracefully turns her prow towards one of the piers, that is crowded with people. What varied emotions fill the bosoms of those there assembled! Some are eagerly, anxiously, expecting the loved wife, from whom they have been separated, perhaps for years; others, dreading, fearing, to meet those whom they have ceased to love, and wish they may never behold again. There were many who had formed connections there that were hard to sever; and among the last named we find Lillie's lover. On the steamer's deck stood his wife, all eagerness to greet her husband after a two years' separation.

The meeting once over, he felt he could sustain his part no longer. Pitiable wife! Henceforth she must be content with a bountiful supply of pocket money. She may revel in luxury, be surrounded with splendor, have every wish gratified but the one yearning desire to possess her husband's love. That was denied to her. She felt the estrangement keenly. What a miserable life was hers! Night after night, as her aching head pressed her lonely pillow, she prayed that death might end her sufferings.

Early morn, perhaps, would bring her husband home. Perchance his only word of salutation would be, "Well, wife, last night I won two, three, or four thousand dollars," just as the case might be; for he was one of those successful gamblers who are well versed in all the tricks used to defraud the unwary. Yes, his coffers were heaped high with his ill-gotten treasures! What cared the wife for riches, if she must ever be treated with that cold, studied politeness, always so freezing to the loving recipient?

Daily I was an unwilling witness to the inward struggles, the pent-up grief, of the proud woman, for we both resided under one roof. She had learned all, everything. Whispered rumors were borne to her ears; and from some source she had learned where was bestowed the affection which of right belonged to her.

In the interim, what had become of Lillie? Had she repented of her sin, and chosen purity's white robe, with which to deck her faultless figure? Ah, no! She did not possess moral courage sufficient to brave the heartless sarcasm, the keen reproach, of that class who are ever ready to judge their fellow-mortals, and who ever forget that divine precept which teaches us that "to err is human; to forgive, divine." And then, after taking the first step in wickedness, it is much easier to follow on in the downward track, than it is to turn, and tread the flowery path of purity, which leads to the mansion of happiness.

After the lapse of a few months, she returned to the inland city; "for," she remarked, "it is some pleasure to breathe the same atmosphere, to traverse the same streets, and frequent the same places of resort as the dearly loved." She rushed recklessly into dissipation. Her extreme beauty, and her adventurous, fearless course of conduct, won for her a widely extended reputation.

One day she would appear in splendid Turkish costume, which admirably displayed her tiny little foot encased in richly embroidered satin slippers. Thus would she promenade the thronged thoroughfares of the city, the observed of all observers. Again she might be seen, superbly dressed after the fashion of that class of people denominated "fast men." How gracefully she held the ribbons, and with what dexterity she managed her spirited horse, as she dashed madly on over the broad plains which surrounded the city. In the use of the cigarita she equalled, in point of fascination, the dark-eyed Spanish women.

I have seen her mounted on a glossy, lithe-limbed race-horse, — one that had won for her many thousands on the course, — habited in a closely-fitting riding-dress of black velvet, ornamented with a hundred and fifty gold buttons, a hat from which depended magnificent sable plumes, and, over her face, a short white lace veil of the richest texture, so gossamer-like, one could almost see the fire of passion flashing from the depths of her dark, lustrous eyes. She took all captive. Gold and diamonds were showered upon her. Her ringing, musical laugh seemed the signal at which trouble, care, and sorrow fled away and hid themselves. Lillie was not soulless, or heartless either; but yet the hilarity of despair seemed to have fast possession of her. Many a tear has fallen at the thought of her sad future.

The unloved wife, finding that all efforts to reclaim her husband's love proved futile, decided to return to the home of her youth. She took passage from San Francisco in a steamer upon which Lillie's mother had also secured her passage; for, despairing of ever reclaiming her daughter, she was hastening to leave a country where so much existed to remind her of her fallen child. Thus were these two sorrowing females thrown together on ship-board; yet neither by word or look did they recognize each other. The mother still cherished the same revengeful feelings towards the seducer; and the proud wife rejected the idea of allowing, even for a moment, the mother of one who unconsciously had been instrumental in causing the sky of her existence to be shrouded in dark, impenetrable gloom, to suspect that she was suffering from unrequited affection.

The husband was happy again with Lillie, until about two years after his wife's departure, when he was unceremoniously hurried into the presence of his Maker. He met his death by the glittering knife of one whom he had defrauded of his last ounce of dust. The one to whom he had done the greatest injury, the most irreparable wrong, wept bitter tears of anguish over his unhonored grave.

There were many beautiful, depraved women in California who, previous to leaving their homes in the Atlantic States, had lived virtuous lives; many who had been the light and the life of the home circle — who had, indeed, been an ornament to the society in which they moved. Some of them were desirous of acquiring riches; and, hearing such glowing accounts of fortunes so speedily amassed in California, and also being possessed of an adventurous spirit, started, as they termed it, to seek their fortunes. Some went with their husbands, some with their fathers, some with their brothers, and too many went alone.

To such as had felt and known all the inconvenience arising from a limited purse, and thought that if they were blessed with riches, or a competency even, their happiness would be complete, — to such, I assert, it was a dangerous country to go to, unless their principles were as firm as the rocks of their native hills.

One beautiful young girl, in company with her brother, left a pleasant home, situated in the heart of the "Old Granite State," and together they reached the El Dorado of the West. He repaired to the mines, after having procured a lucrative situation for his sister as governess in a wealthy Spanish family. Previous to leaving the States, she had been a music teacher.

After awhile, she became tired of her rather monotonous life, and conceived the idea of going to one of the interior cities, to see if she could find something better to do. An offer was made of forty dollars an evening, if she would sit at a Lansquenet table, and deal the cards. At first she shrank with horror at the idea of thus appearing in a gambling-house. Then she thought of her widowed mother at home, deprived of all the comforts and luxuries so acceptable to the middle-aged and feeble. Said she, "What an amount of money I can earn in this way, wherewith to surround mother with every comfort, and yet not compromise my honor in the least!" Mistaken girl! No woman could long remain virtuous in one of those gilded saloons of vice, surrounded, as she must necessarily be, by men who looked upon the opposite sex very much in the same light as does the fish-hawk, which soars above the surface of some clear lake, ever ready to pounce upon, and bear off in its talons, any one of the shining piscatory tribe that, more venturesome than another, approaches too near to the boundaries of its native element.

The night approached on which Jennie was to make her debût in the sporting world. With a palpitating heart, she repaired, in company with her employer, to one of the most magnificent gambling establishments in the city. Upon entering, the dazzling brilliancy of the surrounding appurtenances, the delicious strains of magical music which burst upon her ear, were perfectly enchanting; but, as she raised her eyes to the walls, (from which depended numerous pictures, all calculated to excite the grosser passions of man, and which were inclosed in magnificently gilded frames,) she drank in at a glance her position, and fainted. She was taken to her hotel, and left,.for that night, to her own gloomy reflections.

Oh, Jennie, if you had but listened to, and been guided by, the spirit-influence of your Guardian Angel, who is ever near and ready, unless obstinately resisted, to- soothe the agitated, wavering heart, and, by sweet, whispered breathings of divine counsel, is able to lead the troubled soul to drink of the sweet waters of eternal happiness!

Next morning came the tempter; and, by increasing in amount the already liberal sum proffered for her services, he gained from her a promise to make a second attempt the ensuing evening. She went, and this time succeeded in reaching the seat provided for her; but her head swam, her step faltered; and well it might, for the licentious gaze of hundreds rested admiringly upon her superb figure. Her transcendently beautiful countenance was suffused with the blush of maidenly modesty; and that, having been an unseen and unheard-of feature in such a place, was all the more refreshing for its scarcity.

For some time she retained all her original purity; and then the angels in heaven might have wept, when they saw the tempter secure of his victim. She had launched her skiff upon the sea of immorality, freighted with that priceless treasure, virtue; and, in exchange for which, it had returned to her laden with gold, wherewith she could supply her dearly loved mother's every want. Thus she lived for months; not quite so daring as Lillie, yet drinking sufficiently deep at the Lethean fount to hush all the whisperings of conscience. She finally terminated her profitable career of vice by marrying a wealthy, popular man in one of the mountain towns, — one with whom she had lived on terms of the greatest intimacy for months before their marriage.

She now moves in good society in one of our Eastern cities, surrounded with all the appliances of wealth, in possession of the love of a popular and respected husband. Who, among her numerous friends, would stop to make inquiries of her past life? And, even if her fashionable acquaintances knew of her past follies, I am rather inclined to think they would " wink " at them rather than lose a *wealthy friend.* Such was life as I saw it in California.

CHAPTER XXXII.

Now, kind friends, a few farewell words, and my story closes. On my ride from the depot home, I passed the old, familiar trees; yet, thought I, they have certainly grown smaller. And the brook, too

— why, it was almost dried up; and the hills, how they had diminished in size! I insisted that some of them had been dug away.

There, before me, was the old homestead, the spot where my heart first learned attachment; where my mind had first opened its eyes; where a mother had tenderly nurtured me, from earliest infancy.

How sensibly the shadows of retrospection came creeping over my heart, as I first drew in sight of that endeared place! The roofs and windows looked familiar to my eye; the old trees waved their arms as of yore. I reached the door, raised the latch, and was locked in the embrace of father, mother, brothers. But the sister whom I had left there a light-hearted girl, had gone to gladden and cheer another's home. She had pressed one darling babe to her bosom for a short space; then it had winged its way to blissful realms above, and left the mother desolate.

Now, you have accompanied me on my eventful voyage to California, around Cape Horn, on board burning ships; have sympathized with me in sorrow, joyed with me in pleasure; crossed the Isthmus with me, astride a mule; in fact, followed me through "dangers seen and unseen;" and, finally, reached with me the "old homestead." And, if you have been repaid for the amount of time and patience expended, I am heartily glad of it; and, if you have not, I hope I shall ever remain in "blissful ignorance" of the loss. Good-by!

THE END.

www.ingramcontent.com/pod-product-compliance
Lightning Source LLC
Chambersburg PA
CBHW030003240426
43672CB00007B/801